Shared Treasures

A Journal of Friendship and Fly Fishing

By Sally I. Stoner

Illustrations by Deb J. Cox

Published by
K&D Limited, Inc.
P. O. Box 217
Lisbon, MD 21765-0217
410-489-4967 • kdlimited@rivermyst.net
www.rivermyst.net

ISBN 1-893342-04-2
Library of Congress Cataloging-in-Publication Data
Stoner, Sally I., 1944-
    Shared treasures : a journal of friendship and fly fishing / by Sally I. Stoner ; illustrated
  by Deb Cox.
      p. cm.
    ISBN 1-893342-04-02
    1. Fly Fishing --Anecdotes. 2. Stoner, Sally I., 1944- 3. Cox, Deb, 1953- I. Title.
SH456 .S82 2000
799.1'24--dc211   00-021305

Cover and text design by Donna J. Dove

PRINTED IN CANADA
10   9   8   7   6   5   4   3   2   1

Dedicated to Tanner,
the black cocker spaniel
— who is more than a memory.
— SIS

The illustrations are dedicated
to Katrina, my god-daughter
— also an artist.
— DJC

Acknowledgments

With deep gratitude to friends and family who are the structure on which our lives are built, especially: Carol Mae Florence and Michael Cripe; Ece Malone; Diane and Herb Filipponi; Mary Vickers; Maggie Merriman; Flora Brussa and Patricia Hickey; Sara, Nina, and George Kersels; Bill, Billy, John, and Donna Dove; Marcianne Fast; Cuesta Softball 1995-1998; and the "Women Who Lunch."

Special thanks to the Becoming an Outdoors-Woman program for opening the wonders of the wilderness to so many.

— Sally I. Stoner

I would like to thank Sarah Catlin for her patience and support; my family; Odette Pura and Ethel St. John, whose friendships give me courage; Katrina Pura, a connection that demands that I be my best; Flora Brussa and Pat Hickey, who taught me to be whimsical; Donna Dove; Sally I. Stoner, for the many miles of friendship; and all those with whom I shared the many rivers and streams.

— Deb J. Cox

A Journal

Introduction

There comes a time when the kids are grown, the job promotions disappear and the commute home takes too long. The moment of truth may happen while browsing the Internet, skimming a magazine, or seeing a patch of green whiz by the car window. It's the realization you've lost touch with the natural world. All the concrete and asphalt has boxed your life so completely there is no longer a sparkle of sunlight gleaming off dew moistened petals.

The flash came to me while driving to Montana for my annual fly fishing vacation. The van's windshield was cracked. I was so entangled with my work life and it's associated lack of significance, my vision focussed continuously on the fractured glass instead of the passing world. The imperfection galled me.

On the morning I drove across Raynolds Pass into Montana, my view opened to the huge vista of Big Sky Country. From that moment after, I never saw the crack. My focus lengthened to infinity, to the grand beauty surrounding me. Rather than be diminished by it, I felt my place within it was as important as the highest mountain or the limitless sky. The knowledge of truly belonging to the planet and to even higher energies washed over me. Wading in a cold river with a fly rod reinforced the experience, and redefined my presence in the universe.

When Deb Cox and I teach fly fishing we notice a recurring motivation. Our students want the challenge of mastering a new skill in natural surroundings. Many beginners come to us directly from a harried professional life seeking respite from the constant din of responsibility. They often enroll on their own without a supporting companion. Somehow they find the courage to leave their comfort zone and test themselves in an unpredictable environment. We tell them our stories, share our knowledge, and send them out with encouragement to continue in their powerful journeys. Equally inspired by their bravery, we repay them with gentle guidance into the river's heart.

We see the joy in the faces of those we invite to the stream. After a few hours of being completely enchanted by the process of casting a fly to illusive fish, most beginners emerge from the water with renewed spirits. The furrowed brows and deep lines etched by tension around their eyes are replaced with smiles and voices trilling with enthusiasm. In a transformation as amazing as the metamorphosis of aquatic insects, new anglers find a life giving elixir in the restorative effects of fly fishing.

Out of our experience with teaching, fishing, and telling our stories, we found a way to connect with other people and with our place in the natural world. We also wanted to share our knowledge in a larger context so Deb began her journal of our fly fishing adventures. In her study of history she learned the importance of first person narratives for understanding the past.

More comfortable in a nonverbal form Deb used her artistic talent to chronicle our fly fishing trips. Sketching the theme of the day's adventure with colored pencils, she captured the essence of the experience. She wrote on her journal book plate, "Deb Cox – A Flyfishing Anthology – Shared Treasures."

Deb allowed me to add my own interpretations in poetry and prose, and the book became the creation of two women. An artist and a writer, we are happiest when sharing our passion for fly fishing with others. The stories are relatively chronological, and describe many of the best trout waters in the Western States. They can be read in order or at random. The reader is encouraged to step into the river wherever it looks inviting.

Most of all, whatever sport brings you to the intense and powerful beauty of our Earth, it is important to reestablish a connection with the natural order and the unbridled energy that shapes our universe. Once the relationship is renewed your view will remain on the infinite forever. Within the following words and drawings are glimpses of being fully present in the flow of life's river and our happy invitation to join us there.

Shared Treasures

I grow comfortable
in your arms
breathing easily
in your sweet
embrace

9/6/94
HAT CREEK
P.H. 2

A WONDERFUL DAY ON THE WATER!!
MARY DID REAL WELL, 3 FISH & LANDED ONE ON
HER OWN. ODIE READING IN THE SHADE, SALLY CHANGING
HER FLY... ME RAMRODDING... WE HAD THE WHOLE SECTION OF
THE RIVER TO OURSELVES. MICHELLE HAS ARRIVED & NOW OUR
GROUP IS COMPLETE.

Hat Creek, P.H. 2

Some pieces of water become old friends. Like the girl you've known since kindergarten with whom you've shared both drama and festival. Yours is a comfortable, easy relationship. She comforts you in troubled times and laughs with you at life's surprises. Together since your first memory, she remains constant and forgiving.

Before the Madison River in Montana won my heart, California's Hat Creek was my favorite pal. Our first meeting was in 1979. My friend Lucinda and I became enchanted with fly fishing after reading a magazine devoted to the sport. We knew how to fish, but we were innocents to this enchanting technique. We decided to learn more about the sport. Our education included a pilgrimage to California's best wild trout locale, Hat Creek.

To prepare for our adventure we visited a fly shop in Santa Rosa, our departure point. A jovial shopkeeper sold us starter gear. Not knowing diddily about the sport we purchased what was probably unmarketable to more knowledgeable customers. The rods were heavy fiberglass dinosaurs.

They were difficult to cast and unfriendly to beginners. In the optimism of ignorance and with our newly purchased gear in hand we jubilantly began our expedition.

Hat Creek flowed from the southern Cascade mountain range. Mounts Shasta and Lassen were nearby. First cousins to Mount St. Helens, Lassen has active thermal features and last erupted during the early Twentieth Century. The locale was northeast of major population centers. It was possible then to fish without being jostled by crowds. Local communities were small and functional, and buoyed financially with logging and cattle ranching. The area was ribboned with waters of all classes. Streams, rivers, ponds, lakes, and creeks were plentiful. Most were controlled by a major utility company and used for hydroelectric generation.

Burney, the gateway to Hat Creek and self-professed "full service community," offered an array of accommodations. We chose a modest unit with kitchenette. Settled in, we went in search of knowledge. Finding an affable fellow in a nearby fly shop, we learned a few knots, bought a dozen flies and a few leaders, grabbed a map, and departed for the river.

Babes in the wilderness were we. Cruising north on highway 299 we turned at the small sign which read, "P.H. 2," designating the road to Powerhouse 2. The dusty track wound down in a series of switchbacks past osprey nests built high atop power poles. A final steep descent opened onto a beautiful meadow guarded by the weathered-stone powerhouse perched handsomely on a rocky vertical. Tall transmission towers stood like sentinels guarding the fen. In the foreground Hat Creek curved in a smooth left turn.

It was midweek and only a few fishermen were visible on the stream. Lucinda and I were smitten with the beauty. We took our time wandering along the bank. Hiking behind the powerhouse, we skirted the deeply roiling water roaring from the turbine. The riffle below was easy to wade and tunneled by pines and willows. A spring creek entered on the right after pooling into a large shallow pond. Downstream a hundred yards the river opened into a wider flow broken by islands, boulders, and logs. It was perfect habitat for large rainbow and brown trout.

We walked along the sweeping left bend and were awed by the smooth flat section called Carbon Bridge. Small discreet circles gave notice of trout sipping tiny bugs off the water's surface. Dazzled, we realized the sport would open to us more majestic possibilities than we had reckoned.

Our initial efforts were horrible. Untaught and clumsy, we did our best. We saw fish skitter away from our splashing lines as we kerplunked them on the water. We ripped off dozens of flies on tree branches and thistle weeds. Some we snapped off by popping the end of the monofilament leader like Zorro's whip. What we lacked in prowess we made up in determination. We made a solemn vow to improve our skills so we could give the troutwater its due respect. Lucinda and I kept our promise.

When we returned home, each evening we took our rods to the local high school to practice casting on the soft grass of the football field. We bought books and magazines and immersed ourselves in the mechanics of the sport. In the late spring we enrolled in a streamside class on Hat Creek, and on those same banks learned to cast under the expert tutelage of Maggie Merriman, the best known woman teacher in the country. We hired guides of lesser fame, and eventually began to present the line gently and naturally. Best of all we were catching and releasing trout. In short we cut our fly fishing teeth on Hat Creek.

The two of us attended fly fishing shows and were noticeable by our gender as we walked among a sea of men searching the booths for bargains and information. Often we felt invisible when the vendors looked over our heads to talk to passing men, or gave us only scant attention. Rarely did we encounter other women fishing. Undaunted by female reinforcement we fished on.

We fished earnestly for the next five years. When Lucinda earned a respectable promotion to a position located four hundred miles away, I went recruiting for a new fishing partner. I asked Deb if she was interested in trying the sport. Deb's previous fishing style consisted of tossing a bobber and worm while sitting in a beach chair sipping beer. She was as green as I had been five years earlier. Always game, she agreed to travel to Northeast California. Her parents lived within a few hours drive of Burney. We arranged to meet Lucinda there and travel north together. We camped in a nearby state park and drove to the river for an evening's outing.

Deb was dressed in borrowed waders and red high top tennis shoes. Thick felt was glued on the soles for traction on slippery rocks. There was no need to invest in equipment if she didn't take to the sport. I led her around the powerhouse and through the riffles to the far bank. On the way we noticed small fish rising in the spring-fed pond. A good sign.

We waded into Hat Creek standing quietly among rising fish. I gave her the most rudimentary instructions and she tossed a dry fly across the current. Instantly her rod bent and her reel began to sing. Deb grabbed her rod with both hands and her eyes opened wide. "Now, what do I do?" she gasped.

"Keep your rod tip high and hang on," I replied, staying right by her side. With the luck God gives to beginners, she landed her first trout and several more before the night closed in on us. We returned to the campsite exhausted and thrilled. My old friend, Hat Creek, embraced my new friend.

After such an experience it is almost impossible to go back to one's old fishing ways. We spent a few more days in Hat Creek's company with varying success. Anticipating Deb's acceptance of the sport, I'd booked a three-day float trip on the Deschutes River in Oregon. She honed her skills and was hooked for life.

The next three years we traveled to Hat Creek for spring and fall fishing. Lucinda joined us when she could, but she was climbing the corporate ladder steadily and enjoyed less and less personal time. Each year the parking area held more four-wheel drive vehicles, and the river more anglers. Out of necessity we explored other sections of Hat Creek. We trekked from Highway 299 to the creek's last stretch before it emptied into Lake Britton. We tried nymph fishing techniques, a style of fly fishing disdained by Deb and other dry fly purists. I enjoyed learning fresh techniques and this system was a new trick to add to my bag. Truthfully, I didn't favor it.

We stalked the narrow, shallow waters upstream from Powerhouse 1 competing with bait fishers for hatchery trout. On this portion of Hat Creek we could fish with Deb's parents and take her young nephew into the water without worry. Poring over U. S. Forest Service maps, we found obscure spring creeks to fish in solitude. The grandness of Hat Creek below P.H. 2 always lured us back to its sweet waters.

One June morning Deb became hypothermic while fishing the far bank. She knew she was cold, but before she could leave the water trout began to feed. Staying for just a few more casts proved costly to her body temperature. Emerging from the creek almost too frozen to walk, she stumbled back around the powerhouse to the van. She was visibly in trouble. I quickly removed her waders and warmed her with blankets, while stuffing M&M's into her mouth to fuel her cold furnace. It took her three days to recover. After her frightening episode with the cold, she bought neoprene waders for protection.

On our last trip to Hat Creek we gathered a small, enthusiastic group of women eager to learn the sport. Mary, Odette, and Michelle camped with us for a few days and practiced their new skills in the waters around Burney. We were, as usual, remarkable in our gender make-up. Our group was undoubtedly the largest accumulation of women to fish Hat Creek. They loved the surroundings as much as they enjoyed the sport. The women took time out of the river to lie in the sun-warmed grass reading and napping. They found the same pleasure in the beautiful surroundings as I had on my first visit.

Twenty years after our first meeting, Hat Creek and I have seen many changes. The sturdy old powerhouse may have a new owner, the parking area is even larger, and the trout are wiser. The years have turned my hair silver and my hands crooked. I'm not so apt to wade the strong current just above the islands.

Hat Creek is where it began for me. Along her banks I found a passion which would sustain and nurture me through both painful and joyous challenges. The stream showed me the steps to recovery. It slaked my thirst with beauty and rewarded my sobriety with the dance of magnificent trout. And she worked her same magic for Deb.

Whenever I return to Hat Creek, as the van creeps slowly down the last steep incline, the sight of the stream always takes my breath away. It never fails to thump my chest with the same emotion as coming home to an old, dear friend.

Within the
     small confines
of inhalation
     life
  breathes

CABIN 4 ... 6.8.93
SLOW FISHING DAY — BUT THE WEATHER IS IMPROVING. FIRST SUN IN 4 days!
HAPPY B-DAY DEWEY

Cabin 4

I belong to the rare American breed of creatures who rarely shop in big box stores. Those enormous warehouses stacked to dizzying heights with huge containers of chocolate chips and shampoo overwhelm my particular species. As silly as it may sound, I've spent hours filling the gigantic cart with more goodies than a small country can consume in a year, tossing in twenty pounds of jerky on top of thirty pair of socks, beside four automobile tires, and a complete set of wrenches. When suddenly it dawned on me, I could neither eat nor store any of it, and I backtracked through the boulevard-like aisles returning the stuff to the shelves. More isn't necessarily better.

For years Deb and I were content to spend our fishing expeditions within the small confines of the red van. The first trips were made in a classic 1969 VW camper. Not a pop-up, it was a mud brown color and ten years old when Deb bought it. Although it didn't have rainbows or daisies painted on it, the first time she slammed on the brakes she was surprised when a baggie of marijuana came flying out from under the dash. Pleasantly, I might add.

During one particularly ragged time in her life, she and Tanner, the black cocker spaniel, lived in the small van, happy to have such a comfortable shelter. Several years later when her life turned to happier pursuits, we drove that air-cooled bus of hers all the way to British Columbia. We fished and played golf every chance we got. I knew the idiosyncrasies of the small-engine bus, having driven a similar vehicle for a year through Europe. Underpowered and slowed considerably by head winds and the aerodynamics of passing trucks, the VW began to lose its charm as we aged.

Finally, on one hot, windy trip I got fed up cooling myself with a spray bottle and wrestling the bus back on the road after sixteen wheelers zoomed past. "Enough," I whimpered and headed to the Chevy dealer for an air-conditioned V-8 with power steering. The red van came completely empty except for the two front seats. Deb designed the perfect fishing mobile, which did not include shag carpeting. Easily cleaned surfaces were necessary for muddy fishers and wet dogs. Wood paneling and vinyl were the best materials for the van's future expeditions. The maiden voyage would be our first trip to Montana.

By comparison the new red van seemed like the Taj Mahal. There was room to dance. Not really, but the power and heft of the vehicle coupled with the snazzy rims Deb added to the wheels, made traveling stylish and comfortable. Each trip we added a little modification or a small adaptation to fit our traveling requirements. When we weren't fishing, it was Deb's ride.

Deb named it "Shone" and people began to recognize her cruising around town in her shiny red van. She was always singing along with the tape deck as carefree as a bird. Yet, her life was beginning to change in dramatic ways. After spending much of her youth sowing serious wild oats, Deb was a sober, sole proprietor of a small business, working hard to create a successful niche in the community. A self-taught draftsperson, her business fluctuated directly with residential building trends, and in 1988 home construction in California was plummeting. Not one to accept a passive stance, she decided to take classes at the community college. She chose an American History course and enrolled.

She loved the lecture and her professor. She attended night classes twice a week. From the first assignment Deb struggled with the reading. Deb grew up in a small farming town in the Salinas Valley during the educational experiment in new ways to teach reading. Sadly, the modern methods left some children behind, and in a rural system there was no room for remediation.

What she lacked in reading aptitude, she made up for in personal skills. In other words she became quite good at faking it. As we all do in our child's mind, when we find ourselves without the same tools as other kids we decide we are inferior and adopt some compensating mechanism.

During her first history class it all came home to roost. It took Deb an hour to read a page of text. Sometimes the tears would quietly slide down her cheeks as she looked up word after world in her small, paperback dictionary. Tenacious and determined, she plodded on. Her reward was receiving the highest grade in the class and the admiration of her professor.

Deb realized it would take an Herculean effort to finish a degree program at her exceedingly arduous pace. She felt in her secret heart she wasn't smart enough, which was far from true. Then, during a fishing trip to Kings River, our guest on the outing told Deb about a reading tutor. Our friend's young son was struggling to read and she augmented his school lessons with a local tutor, whose methods proved so effective her son accelerated rapidly. Held in high regard within the educational community, the tutor was known for her outstanding success with all ages of students.

It was all Deb needed to know. The red van was barely parked in the driveway and she was on the phone making an appointment for an evaluation. She started the program immediately. Deb worked hard learning phonetics and for the first time knowing how to determine the sounds in a word. The results were amazing, and she started reading everything in sight. More importantly, she realized she was as smart as others. A bright light went on in her heart.

When the residential construction industry fell to new lows, Deb's business slowed to a trickle. Her concentration shifted to her education.

She enrolled as a full-time student including summer sessions at the local community college. Our fishing adventures now were planned around the school calendar. In 1993, she graduated second in her class and was accepted at the local university.

Montana in late May can be cold and rainy. Our solution to the risky weather was to rent a cabin. We were accustomed to small quarters, so one room with a cook stove, refrigerator, and indoor plumbing seemed like a penthouse. Cabin 4 was perfect. Knotty pine and clean as a whistle, it had a small table tucked into a shed dormer where we could play our marathon gin rummy games. From the same vantage point we watched the comings and goings of everyone in camp, who were few at that time of the season.

If the red van seemed like a mansion, Cabin 4 was a palace. We hung our fishing vests on crucially placed nails, bought a cute little table cloth, and set the radio in the window tuned to the country station from Idaho Falls. There was comfort in our dry, warm space and we learned to be at peace within ourselves and the wonderful room.

We fished in the snow and freezing rain. From our window we watched the thunderstorms pound the snow-covered mountains. Admittedly, we felt a bit smug being brave enough to venture out in a snow flurry to fish the frigid waters for torporous trout. Deb even bought a fleece-lined wool cap with earflaps to wear on the river. It wasn't a charming fashion statement.

She looked like Elmer Fudd, but it kept her head from freezing. Knowing we could get dry and warm in our cabin gave us the sense of security we needed to test the elements.

As the weather warmed, the fishing improved, but a good bug hatch was still a few weeks away. Cabin Creek came tumbling down from the higher elevations, the color of Deb's old van. Its muddy waters made the Madison unfishable downstream. Our favorite runs near Hebgen Dam were high and fast, and we found new pools and pockets where big trout lurked in the early summer cold. We experienced Montana in a new, exciting way.

It is easy in this life of ours to want more things and bigger spaces, as if we can fill the hollows of our hearts with stuff. Even Deb and I added room and some small opulence to our outdoor adventures. Yet the austere luxury of Cabin 4 was a direct result of a deeper lesson.

We were enjoying the shelter of a warm cabin and hot shower because of Deb's refusal to accept defeat and her tenacity in overcoming an inadequate education. Out of her courageous effort to learn more about the world, our accompanying benefit was the comfort of Cabin 4.

It's impossible to know what will come if we stop choosing fear, or realize more stuff can never fill an empty heart. I do know Deb graduated Summa Cum Laude and continued her graduate study at the University of California Santa Barbara. And in the early summer of 1993, she trounced me solidly at gin rummy.

Looking up
   through
   sycamore branches
your sunburned face
     warms
   my day

6.13.93...

WHAT A DAY — I COULDN'T ASK FOR ANYTHING MORE ... BLUE SKY, BEST FRIENDS & GOOD
FISHIN — SALLY HOOKED A MONSTER, EFFIE LANDED A 18" BOU & SO DID PAT.
ONE LANDED 1 & HOOKED MANY

What A Day

Few things are more unpredictable than groups of people. There are entire college departments and large corporations whose sole objective is to describe the oddities of a collection of humans. Politicians and marketeers commission studies to forecast the behavior of their particular target audience. They rely on the information to turn the tide in their favor.

If you have ever thrown a party and invited all the folks you love and adore, you realize just how difficult it is to know what the chemistry will be. It's always a surprise how the revelers interact. Frequently, your best friends can't stand each other. Or after spending a weekend with a few of your closest buddies, it is amazing to discover what dolts they are.

It is a wonderful accident of nature when a handful of women as different as the League of Nations comes together in harmony and accord. Magically, Deb and I managed to assemble a few of these happy groups. Our bunch this year came to fish and as their gillies (Scottish term for fishing guide) we were determined to provide them with the best possible experience.

We introduced them to the sport of fly fishing and were a bit non-plussed when each one showed a passion to continue. The Madison River was the ideal teaching river. Within an easy walk from the cozy cabins along the river were an infinite variety of angling challenges. From novice to expert the water offered the right degree of difficulty for all comers.

Deb and I are very different in our teaching and fishing styles. Her casting form is rhythmic and classy, while mine is overpowered and gruff. I try to learn as many knots as possible and she relies on a few all-purpose ties. My need to know applies to strategies and fly patterns. Deb is happy to catch trout. More a purist than I, she prefers casting a dry fly to feeding fish so she can watch the high floating feathers be attacked by an eager trout. She is the fishing example of student surpassing teacher. We are both big show-offs.

Our differences make for good instruction. Beginners have the opportunity to take the best from each of us and to adapt it to their own emerging skills. It also is an emphatic example of the individualization of the sport. There is no one right way. An angler can bring her own uniqueness to her fishing as long as the result is effective. What Deb and I share most deeply is our strong intention for our group to enjoy their experiences.

Our gang for these few days had very busy lives. Pat, or Trish as her family calls her, was a single mother with a pre-teen son who was active in sports. Her job required many overtime hours but she made parenting her number one priority. Being away from home for a few days was a guilty pleasure for her. The most experienced angler of the three, she needed the least attention. Trish was very serious and focused when on the water. In the evening she preferred to read rather than join our ruthless games of Pedro, a card game brought to California by the Portuguese.

Odette and Deb grew up in the same Central California agricultural community. Although their backgrounds were very different, they shared the commonality of place. Odie was raised on a vast cattle ranch. The oldest of three sisters, she had the quiet efficiency of an eldest child. Her third grade teacher had picked Odie to marry her son when she first called her name in class. She did and they have three small children including a set of twins. Her husband, Randy, having excelled at Stanford and Harvard enjoyed a successful career. Odie relished being a full-time mother. Before the babies came along she taught elementary school like her mother-in-law and studied art.

Odette was avid about fly fishing. She fished with the fire she brought to any endeavor. Her own worst critic, she worked at the skill of casting and would stay on the river until we sent the posse out after her. Intent on hooking fish, she reacted so quickly to the take she pulled the fly right out of the fish's mouth. When at last she solidly hooked one she would hold her breath while playing a spunky trout. One of our important chores as gillies was to remind her to breathe. It was a common occurrence to hear one of us shouting across the river, "Breathe, Odie, breathe."

A fierce competitor in every activity, Odette played cards in the same take-no-prisoners way. As sweet and genteel as she was in everyday life, when given a contest she was no-holds-barred. At our first meeting she crushed me in a game of Pedro. She and Deb were always partners when we played four handed.

Ethel and I were partners. Whether it was pinochle or Pedro we were dealing, I confused her. She couldn't predict my playing strategy. Sometimes I played recklessly and other times with caution. Effie on the other hand played every card game as if it were bridge. She calculated every move and figured probabilities. Ethel was intentional about everything.

It surprised me how much she loved to fly fish. She was just as deliberate on the water as she was playing cards. Effie could stand in one spot for hours without tedium for it. I teased her about wearing the fish down with her steadfast effort. Her first visit to the Madison River was with her husband, Jim. One evening we were fishing off Flora's Point when Effie hooked a big, strong rainbow trout. The fish leaped out of the water and turned downstream swimming with the speed of a jet boat. Effie stood motionless and quietly asking for suggestions. Meanwhile, I was hopping around shrieking like a wild woman, giving instructions and cussing at the size of the trout. Then she said without inflection, "I think my reel is coming off."

I grabbed the reel before it slipped into the river, reattached it to her rod while she held the trout steady. Calmly, she landed a twenty-inch rainbow trout. Almost more than the activity, Ethel loved the sport for it's surrounding beauty. Often, it was an interruption in her musing to hook a fish. She didn't lose fish. Once the set was hard she patiently worked the fish to net. Enjoying adventure she tried anything. She wasn't a pushover. If it didn't suit her she was candid with her dislike but never rancorous.

On this day's outing every woman found a perfect spot on the Madison to cast, mend and recast. There were trout and whitefish eager to grab a tasty-looking feathered imitation. It was early in the season. The river was high and loaded with food.

Trish agreed to wade with me arm in arm across the swift water to an island. She was a strong-legged woman and we crossed the current carefully. Reaching the outer channel of the grassy island, we found big fish working in the deep feeding lanes. I followed behind letting her have the first cast. She was into good fish immediately and landed a sizeable trout. It was contrary to her sport fishing background to release a good fish, but under my frowning gaze she returned the fish to the river unharmed. I hooked and lost a large rainbow trout. Calling it a "long distance release" I pretended flimsily I did it on purpose, convincing no one.

Deb stayed on the bank with Odette and Ethel assisting them with their tackle and helping them read the water locating feeding fish. Too busy to fish, she leaned her rod against a tree and gave the women her full attention. The morning flew by in the quickness of pleasure.

Our group was not perfect and after one more outing, Trish opted out. We added new members and tried other card games. The heart of our group—Ethel, Odette, Deb, and I—fished together for several more seasons before the unpredictable circumstances of life led us in other directions. For this day it was a delicious mix, spiced just right with flavors rich and succulent.

What Deb and I learned from teaching our friends, we applied to the Becoming an Outdoors-Woman program. Introducing more women to the sport and to our own diverse styles, we came to love teaching almost as much as fly fishing. Like all groups, our BOW classes typically have their own characteristics, but somehow we always manage to make them laugh. And, best of all, we get to show off as much as we want.

Your shoulders
     are my grandstand
your arms
     become my home
 in your soul
     my dreams
       find me

6.14.93... THE FIRE HOLE, NEZ PERCE & TATONKA... BEAUTIFUL DAY... DRY FLIES...
SMALL RAINBOW & A BROWN WERE CAUGHT... PEANUT BUTTER & JELLY

The Firehole, Nez Perce & Tatonka

I sobbed all the way through "Dances with Wolves." It was a Sunday afternoon and a group of friends decided to go to the movie. Our Central California town had a wonderful old-fashioned theater which had been lovingly restored. The Art Deco façade warmly invited a viewer to a few hours eating freshly made popcorn while comfortably seated in a cozy reclining seat. It was a perfect way to spend a cold spring afternoon. Unless your hormones were twisting you.

Everything in the film made me cry. The colors in the sky, the wolf, the horse, the Lakota braves, Stands With Fist— all brought streams of tears flooding down my face. Even the great thundering stampede of buffalo caused my lower lip to quiver. "Tatonka," grunted Kevin Costner using his fingers to create the horns of the creature. "Tatonka," the chief growled back, and I cried as communication between the two characters began.

The intensity of emotion was disproportional to the screen play, but I sank lower in my cushy chair and soaked more tissues. When the show was finally over, I could barely walk. Spent and soggy, I stumbled slowly out of the theater and went directly home to bed. My friends wondered about my sanity.

After seeing the movie Deb started calling the huge, shaggy animals freely roaming the wilds of Yellowstone National Park, Tatonka. To her the Lakota word was truer to the animal than the confused English designation, which was either bison or buffalo. Maybe it was the way the tongue hit the back of the teeth when making a "t" sound giving the word a stronger trill than the effete, lip-generated "buh" noise. Whatever the reason, the name caught on with us and we used the Lakota word, Tatonka, thereafter.

In the past I fished among cattle. Mostly cows and steers; infrequently a bull might be pastured beside a trout stream, and I always gave him the respect he commanded. The large, benign, bovines were environmental hazards to the trout habitat because their hoofs eroded the bank, but their company was peaceful.

Tatonka, on the other hand, is not a domesticated animal. When the big, furry, critter wanders near your fishing space, it can be a little touchy. In Yellowstone Park it happens regularly and anglers learn to be ever vigilant in those waters.

The first buffalo sighting for Deb and me was appropriately enough at Buffalo Ford in the Hayden Valley of Yellowstone Park. We were among the many other motorists pulled over to the side of the roadway to gawk as two young bulls engaged in a small territorial dispute. We watched fascinated as the animals pawed and snorted. Suddenly one bull turned in the direction of the van. We decided to beat a hasty retreat. Certainly the big, red vehicle was having the same effect on the bison bull as a matador's cape in a Spanish ring. Neither of us wanted those thick pointy horns stuck in the side of the Chevy.

Avoidance has ever after been the watchword when it comes to Tatonka. Around the Firehole River seemed to be a favorite grazing area for bison. As the smooth, clear river flowed slowly past steaming fumaroles and sulfur pots it curved through a vast meadow before the smaller creek, the Nez Perce, mixed with its waters. During the early summer the water was still crispy cold and the brown trout beckoned.

Deb and I liked to fish the quiet depths of the Firehole and the small riffles of the Nez Perce before the tourist season sprang into full tilt. We would scout for Tatonka before choosing a parking place, not wanting to fish too far from the van in case we had to run for it. If the herds were settled into the meadow we'd drive past the river and proceed to Old Faithful, have lunch, and check again on our way home.

A visit to Yellowstone Park was never disappointing, even if it meant no fishing. Some trips to the Nez Perce were cut short when a juvenile bull came sauntering along the creek en route to some greener glade. We would have to abandon casting to feisty brown trout. I'd hear Deb screaming my name, and I'd look up to see her waving her arms while scampering for the safety of the van. Reluctantly, I'd reel in my line, fasten my elk hair caddis fly to my hook keeper and scurry after her.

When friends would join us in Montana, we always included a trip to the Firehole in their itinerary. It was such a beautiful spot and easy to fish even for beginners. In the early summer of 1993, we were playing host to Odette, Ethel, and Trish. Women to whom we had introduced the sport of fly fishing. The weather had been rainy and cold, but the day we ventured into Yellowstone was sunny.

We drove in from West Yellowstone and cruised along the Madison River watching for elk, moose, bear, or swans. It was five years after the devastating fire had roared through the Park and the vegetation regrowth was slow but encouraging. Turning south toward Old Faithful, we kept a sharp look out for animals and anglers. When we stopped to fish along the Firehole it was late morning and we had a long stretch of river to ourselves. Tatonka was a safe distance away on the far side of the meadow.

We parked off the road and began to assemble our gear. It was still cold enough for long underwear as a first layer. In any outdoor activity dressing properly is necessary for comfort and an important safety concern.

Hypothermia can be the dangerous result of inadequate clothing. We added waders, boots, and several layers of shirts before waddling into the water. Some of the group actually managed to look fashionable in their garb. It was all in their accessories, which were brightly colored neckerchiefs.

Deb took Odie down to a small run of riffles and started her casting upstream into the broken water. She enticed a few brown trout to look at her mayfly imitation, but she was still missing the strike. I took Ethel to a smoother section and pointed out a feeding seam for her to work. Trish went off upstream. She liked to be away from the group. I hollered to her to watch for Tatonka.

After a few hours fishing the Firehole we moved over to fish the waters of the Nez Perce. There was a quiet picnic spot maintained along the creek and it was time for lunch. A group of saffron-robed Buddhist monks were also picnicking there. They were excited to snap our photos as part of their Yellowstone adventure. We obliged demurely.

As was our habit, Deb and I left our tackle in the van to be streamside assistants. We tied on flies and untangled line in the best gillie tradition. When fishing Yellowstone waters a gillie's responsibility includes Tatonka watch, but for this day's outing the animals obliged us by staying out of anxious range. They were close enough to be exciting, and far enough to be unthreatening. We could relax on the creek bank. Eating our peanut butter sandwiches, watching the small trout take bugs off the surface, we let the sun warm our bare arms as the afternoon melted away.

The exquisite beauty of Yellowstone National Park is unsurpassed in its magnificence. It is all the more magical when you become part of the environment. Wading the slow, strong current of the Firehole River or walking carefully along the bank of the Nez Perce watching for the flash of a feeding trout brings you within its vibrant circle of energy.

Even better is the privilege of sharing the experience with friends and being present when they spot their first moose or hook their first brown trout. Sometimes the most memorable event of an outing is the quiet, sun-warmed enjoyment of a peanut butter and jelly sandwich savored within view of grazing Tatonka.

Maybe it was the same kind of simple beauty that evoked such deep emotion when I watched "Dances with Wolves." I've never attempted to see it again. I'm content to let the memory of it stay untainted and, out of reverence, refer to bison as Tatonka.

"Too green,"
    she said
"Montana,"
    she meant
        no need
    for other
words

6.16.93... FISHIN THE
GALLATIN RIVER ON A
COLD, CLOUDY DAY... WE
BEAT IT HARD BUT NOT MUCH
ACTION... ODIE & I FLUSHED OUT A
HUGE MOOSE... GOOD TO BE FISHIN WITH
FLORA

Gallatin River

It is humanly impossible to travel without forming an opinion. A place once visited elicits descriptive words beyond the anonymous inscription on post cards. A vista is wide and magnificent, green and lush, or dark and ominous. Locales are inviting, quaint, curious, or lackluster, and the citizens can be friendly, helpful, or snobbish. To discover the world is to find a favorite in each geographical category.

So far I love Holland, am partial to Canadians, and favor living near the ocean but vacationing in mountains with conifer forests and clear cold trout waters. Of all the roads I've rolled along, Montana's Highway 191 is my most beloved. From its single lane much of what defines Montana's grandeur is viewed.

The road climbs out of the expansive valley surrounding Bozeman and narrows into a gorge following the white water section of the Gallatin River. Rafts and kayaks tumble through the froth challenging paddlers. Roadside crosses mark the tragic end of some journeys.

After winding through the narrow ledges of the gorge, the road bursts out along the sage-sprinkled pastures near Big Sky. Here the mighty Gallatin calmly spreads, and anglers park their rigs to cast fly lines to her legendary depths. The highway curves sensually entering the western edge of Yellowstone Park. Easily accessible to anglers, the river sings and sparkles. Lodge pole forests charred from the terrible fire of 1988, cheek by jowl to healthy green trees, all slide down the tall peaks to the water's edge while moose graze the wetland marshes.

The highway moves away from the Gallatin and partners with the smaller rill of Grayling Creek. The hips of the mountains nudge the asphalt and the sky becomes a small ribbon of light. The road bends to the left and suddenly emerges onto a stunning panorama. A view so enormous and dramatic in scope, it strikes a primal chord in human hearts and they cry out in awe. Even frequent travelers gasp each time they're struck with the sight.

Like most magnificent sensory experiences it is a great joy to share with friends. I love dragging my friends along to places and activities I find thrilling. Sometimes they even enjoy themselves. In 1992, Deb and I brought nine women together to fish the Deschutes River in Central Oregon. A few of them never fished before the trip. For three days we camped in tents along the river we had fished. Our grizzled fishing guides helped us find and hook fish. They cooked huge meals and told us tales of past excursions. The women were enthralled with the complete excursion.

This summer we played host to three of the women whose enjoyment of the river trip sparked a hunger for more fly fishing adventures. Wanting to show them the outstanding angling of Montana, we agreed to be their gillies, as they say in Scotland. The trio flew into Bozeman which meant a drive south on Highway 191 was their introduction to Western Montana. With difficulty I concentrated on driving while Deb signaled points of interest and spotted wildlife for our enthusiastic passengers.

Of the three, Trish and Ethel were return visitors. They had been charmed by our description of the area and included a trip in earlier vacations. It was Odette's first trip. She was the most seasoned traveler and Deb's oldest friend. Odie, as we called her, took to the sport with her characteristic ferocity. When she found something to her liking she grabbed it with a passionate flair, which made her eyes shoot fire and her entire body lean into the doing of it.

Contrarily, Ethel's approach was quiet and soft. Sometimes I wondered if her feet were touching the ground. She moved in a gliding fashion like a hovercraft and had a way of sighing in mid-sentence as if she were hearing ethereal messages.

Trish was solidly Irish and a serious angler. Her preferred sport was the tougher fishing on the Pacific Ocean, but she acquiesced to join us on the lesser water. She'd arrived a day before the other two and fished happily in a sudden snow flurry.

Although the women differed greatly in appearance and personality, they shared the commonality of motherhood. Ethel enjoyed grandmother status, yet after photos were displayed and updates exchanged, fly fishing was the group's main focus.

Meal preparation was organized and the menus rivaled Julia Child's best. When the evening dishes were cleared, the playing cards appeared. Tequila and vintage wine bottles cluttered the counter. Fishing lies and cutthroat card games were the favored entertainment.

Every morning Deb and I rousted our charges with freshly brewed coffee and herded them off to the river. Deb was like a border collie skillfully moving her flock, and relentless in her duty. The weather was Montana's best variety. There was snow, thunder, lightning, sunshine, wind, and sleet. We fished in all conditions except the lightning, which was too dangerous.

We traveled up Highway 191 to fish the Gallatin. Flora, my college mentor, joined us for the day's outing. Parking along the section within Yellowstone's boundary, we were six women arranging tackle. A woman Park Ranger made a U-turn on 191 to check our licenses. She was surprised to spot such a large group of women anglers, and she was visibly delighted to welcome us to her resource.

The morning was cold and blustery, but our group was game. Trish went down river determined to roll some trout. Deb and Odie flushed a moose. They came sprinting from the underbrush with big wide-eyed grins, breathless from their encounter. The moose went in the opposite direction with the same expression on her face.

I spent time with Ethel standing shin deep in a wide pool. She wanted to practice her presentation and feel the river move against her body. The totality of the experience was what Ethel craved. Being in the river, surrounded by Montana beauty was her joy. On the ride from Bozeman as I negotiated the van through the last turn along Grayling Creek, Ethel turned to Odette and quietly said, "If I knew I only had a short time to live, I would come here to spend my last days."

Hearing her candid revelation startled me. I came close to leaving the road astonished by her reverence for the place I held dear. She and I were so different, but our friendship was steadfast. I was frequently amazed by her peaceful strength. Most of the time I felt like a chicken-head eating geek next to her placid composure, while other moments she made my chest puff with complimentary exclamations. "You are a very good teacher," she told me and I'd stand a little taller. Ethel never realized the impact of her blessings.

The Gallatin River taunted our group that morning. Cold, changeable weather kept the fish torpid. Yet, as always, there were unexpected delights to fill the day's memories: a sudden encounter with a moose, a Park Ranger's enthusiastic recognition of our group, and the simple act of breathing the crisp Montana air. Being together along Highway 191, enveloped by a land so exquisite, nullified the absence of trout activity.

Deb, alone, managed to coax a few persnickety fish to grab her fly. She was uncannily fortunate when fishing with a group. It is entirely possible she knew a secret prayer which when uttered under her breath would appease the Great Trout Goddess and success would be bestowed. Or the sheer power of her intention caused trout to take her fly at the most opportune moments. Just as a particularly obnoxious guide would float by with a boat full of clients, Deb would invariably hook a monster rainbow trout. The fish would further oblige her by leaping high out of the water and sticking out its tongue at the passing anglers.

Today, her reputation remained in tact. She teased us good-naturedly about our lack of piscatorial acumen as we ambled back to strip down our gear for the ride to the Madison. Knowing the nature of Montana weather, the sun might be shining at camp and we might fish in shirtsleeves during the afternoon. Regardless, we would eat a sumptuous meal, play a ruthless game of cards, and laugh at our own stories.

Deb and I, the gillies, checked gear and tied leaders, so our anglers would be ready for their next turn on the river. When the adventure was too soon over, the first leg of the journey home took them back along Highway 191. Even though the ride was heavy with the reluctance of ending a joyful trip, the land they passed was magnificent and would remain forever a vibrant memory.

What enchanted
journey
moved
your unassuming
gaze
to my smile?

JUNE 22

SALLY WOKE UP W/ MORE FACE THAN SHE WENT TO SLEEP WITH, SO I HAD
TO FISH BY MYSELF... WENT LOOKING FOR THE BIG BROWN AT FLORA'S PT. I
FOUND HIM UNDER A BOULDER BUT HE WAS NOT INTERESTED IN MY
FLIES. SALLY LOOKS & FEELS MUCH BETTER. PAINTED W/ PAT... MUCH FUN!

Big Brown

Anglers are quirk ridden. We are a superstitious lot, whose success in hooking fish is dependent on a bunch of odd things. So we think. The check list could include: a grimy old hat; a tattered shirt; a vest that has never seen the inside of a washer; an unraveling fly attached to some piece of apparel. Anything can be considered lucky. A pin, a rod, a fly box, even underwear can be a fisher's secret for catching a trophy.

In the same eccentric fashion we play favorites. We like some kinds of fish better than others. The most popular species have volumes written about their specialness, and myths and legends are created for them. Traditionally, fly fishers stalk trout. The sport was first described five hundred years ago by Dame Juliana Berners as a prescription for a happy old age. In her writing, fly fishing was only one of six ways to angle for a variety of fish, but the treatise is still the most frequently quoted in the context of fly fishing.

Because her description was written in Britain, the quarry trout were most likely brown. One of the most sought-after even now, the brown trout is always referred to as, "a big brown trout." For reasons unknown there is no such thing as an iddy biddy brown trout. Apparently they are hatched from the egg already giant. According to late night campfire lore, they are the most elusive of their ilk.

Not truly brown in color, the fish is a yellowish hue with scattered red dots along its side. As it grows to maturity, the male's lower jaw becomes elongated and hooks upward giving the fish a very mean look – a piscine characteristic lending credibility to the general myth.

My earliest recollection of brown trout is of dead, hook-jawed, monsters displayed in a cold box outside a sporting goods store in Bishop, California. Caught by some lucky fisherman on his special lure, the evil giants were thoroughly studied by my brother and me. We leaned our chins on the side of the frozen case and dreamed of bent rods and long battles. Our reverie interrupted by the cranky shop owner shooing us, we walked away creating our own mystic brown trout stories.

On the small Sierra creek where we fished for hatchery raised trout, occasionally we'd hook a fish that was not a rainbow. My uncle called them "Loch Levens." The fish had red spots and were small. We never imagined those six inchers were remotely related to the kiped-jawed uglies in the freezer. My uncle knew all there was to know about fish and referred to the big brown trout as German Browns.

60

The foreign designations added to the allure of the brown trout. German and Scottish heritages brought a rather cosmopolitan flair to the quest for brownies. When I grew older and wiser in all things trout, I learned the fish were imported to the U.S. from both countries. An intentional act I found amusing. It evoked a mental image of a kilt-clad fisherman nudging a lederhosen-adorned buddy remarking in a thick brogue, "Ach, laddie, what this country needs is a fine brown trout."

As I matured into the sport, my knowledge deepened. I learned more about the fish and the aquatic insects on which they fed. The wonderful bugs we tried to imitate with feathers and fur to lure the energetic fish were a study in entomology. I also learned brown trout were truly elusive. They liked to skulk under logs and undercut banks, usually taking a fly when it was too dark to tell just what sort of fish was attacking your offering. They seldom came flying out of the water but dove deep when hooked. Brownies knew to wrap a line around logs or rocks to break it off. If the tactic proved fruitless they swam straight toward you at the speed of light, making it impossible to keep a taut line. With any small slack, the brown would be gone. Yet, when all their tricks were played and you were still the boss, they came rather easily to net.

The brilliantly colorful rainbow trout is my favorite. She's a dancer and an acrobat with the strength to run and leap when she should be tuckered. The rainbow is a native American trout, and has been adapting to her home waters for millennia. Her colors vary with the water she swims and can be bright crimson to almost silver. A discerning species, she can not survive in an adverse neighborhood, and her disappearance signals trouble for the habitat. I've never seen an ugly rainbow trout.

Brown trout are home bodies. When they find a place to their liking, they tend to stay put. If an angler entices a nice brown to take her proffered artificial but misses the strike, it's almost certain the brown will be there for a second go.

On this particular trip to Montana I was nursing an abscessed tooth, laid low with the kind of pain that makes you contemplate getting the pliers and extracting the culprit yourself. I was unfit for streamside ventures. The closest dentist was 90 miles away in Bozeman and the appointment was made. In the meanwhile I holed up eating handfuls of aspirin and feeling sorry for myself.

Deb played nurse as long as she could tolerate the constant moaning. Finally she broke out of Cabin 4 with rod in hand and took off running toward Flora's Point. It is never a wise idea to fish alone. Every season so-called expert anglers are lost forever on solo trips. One misstep in a swift river and you're a goner. Deb, however, is not foolhardy. She let a few people in camp know where she was going and when to expect her return. Promising me she would only take the easy wade to Flora's Point, she was gone.

Tanner, the black cocker spaniel, was happy to stay with me snoozing comfortably on the bed. It was a warm Montana summer day and I was sorry not to be on the river. Deb walked the short distance through camp and down the steep bank to the Madison River. Lowering herself into the slower shallows on the highway side of Tanner's Island, it wasn't a difficult wade to the tailout water down river from the island.

At this point the Madison makes a wide sweeping bend. There are deep pockets holding big fish toward the middle of the stream. On the road side there are a series of boulders where Deb knew a big brown trout lurked among the tumble. She waded slowly and quietly, bent forward slightly at the waist in the typical fly fisher posture. Wearing polarized sunglasses to cut the glare off the water, she looked for the brown trout's lair.

She spotted the big fish finning in the slower current behind a boulder. Choosing a favorite dry fly, Deb made a cast just upstream and let the elk hair caddis drift smoothly past the brown. A look was all the fish gave. She cast again and watched the high-floating fly bob naturally past the brownie. Big brown didn't even swish a fin.

Deb is particularly tenacious when she can see a trout. She pulled in her line and tied on a different fly. She chose a bright colored stimulator. Big, buggy, and delicious looking, it had no effect on the big brown. Next she tried a wet fly, an imitation weighted slightly, and fished under the surface. After two or three dead drifts her frustration level rose dramatically.

In desperation and with a teaspoon of sheer meanness, Deb tied on the biggest, heaviest fly in her box. Knowing the big brown was not going to glance at it, she used the fly to bonk the trout on its head. The big brown remained motionless even with her harassment.

A fish versus woman stand-off. Finally, piqued, Deb gave in to her frustration, acknowledged the brown trout as champion, and returned to camp to pursue more artistic endeavors.

She knew there were future opportunities to cast to the big brown trout. Or maybe another angler would be lucky enough to have a go at the fish. Hopefully, if the big brown was hooked, the fisher would return it to the river. If not, chances were another fish would find the boulder and settle in. A good hole was a good hole for any fish big enough or smart enough to claim it.

The brown trout of the Madison River in Montana are now referred to as "native" trout. No longer called German or Scotch they are bred and hatched in the pristine waters of the Mississippian tributary. The legend of the big brown trout grows with each hooked fish. As the myth enlarges, so does the popularity of the fish. Who knows? Maybe one day anglers will be spotted fishing in kilts or leather shorts. Of course, it will be their lucky fishing outfit.

Washed by sudden rain
wildflowers
unbend soft petals
shining toward the
sun

7-12-95

MORE THUNDER, LIGTHING, &
RAIN... LOTS OF RAIN! OF
COURSE OUR ADDITION IS
FLAT AGAIN!! FLORA, JEAN,
SALLY, & I FISHED FLORA'S
PT AREA, SALLY CAUGHT A NICE
BOW IN FRONT OF SOME MEN THAT
HAD BEEN BEATING THE WATER
FOREVER!! FLORA & JEAN HAD
GOOD LUCK... MORE PEOPLE FISHIN
FLORA'S PT BECAUSE OF WHIRLING
DISEASE. MADE A FAST TRIP
TO W.Y. THE RAIN KEEPS US
INSIDE & COZY... SPENDING
Some quality time. THE
BOYS ARE IN
HEAVEN. THIS
BIRD IS FOR
PAT!!

BELTED
KINGFISHER

Belted Kingfisher

Montana is a true test of strength for almost anything. Animals, geology, people, gear, and relationships are bombarded by extraordinarily rugged natural forces. Winters in the beautiful state are notorious for their ferocity, and summer days can begin sweetly mild and within minutes a tornado will snap a grove of Aspens like toothpicks. A favorite local saying goes, "If you don't like the weather now, wait ten minutes and it will change."

For anglers having solid walls for shelter against the vagaries of the weather is a welcomed luxury. Deb and I were no exception. When our scheduled time in Montana fell early in June one year, we rented a small, cozy cabin anticipating the colder weather. We liked it so much we continued to rent the little cabin until the acquisition of a second dog, Buster, was a strain on the "no pets in cabins" rule.

After the comfort of Cabin 4, we were reluctant to go back to the tight quarters of camping in the red van with two dogs. The solution was a borrowed tent trailer. Small, easy to tow, and without frills, the loaner rig was a perfect camping home for women and dogs. It boasted an additional screen room which we used as a kitchen, dining room, and afternoon lounge. The mesh walls kept noxious, biting insects from attacking a snoozing angler while she napped near the banks of the Madison River.

As convenient as the added space was, the screen room suffered from poorly thought-out engineering. Obviously the designer had very little camping experience, and never tried to erect the flimsy structure in a Montana breeze. It was not difficult to put together after we practiced a few times. Four poles, a little hook and loop, and voilà, a convenient, airy, bug-resistant space was attached to the side of the tent trailer.

In reality the screen room was an enclosed awning. It could also be used without the sides for shade. The oddity of its construction was the lack of substantial attachment for the top to the supporting poles. The canvas awning, which was the top, simply rested on the poles. The slightest air current could lift the entire piece of material up, up, and away. Since the support poles were not securely tethered but were essentially held in place by the weight of the awning, when the top took off the poles fell down. Whereupon the sides caved in with the poles and the entire structure crumpled to the ground in a confusing heap. Or, more exciting was when, during a typical Montana afternoon, a zephyr would waft through the campground, the sides would become sails and fly across into the next campsite.

Another pesky aspect of the screen room was the capacity for the roof/awning to hold gallons of water during a rainstorm. The resultant accumulation would further stress the skimpy construction. When one drop too many fell into the small roof pond, the addition collapsed, usually simultaneously with one of us stepping out to check the integrity of the room. Not only would we get drenched by the resulting waterfall, but it was a struggle to reassemble the dripping structure as the blustery thunderstorm continued. Finally, we got smart. When the slightest inkling of a brisk or rainy interlude threatened, Deb disassembled the screen room before the storm did.

We got our first hint about the rig immediately after setting up our beautiful camp along the Madison. There were several steps to unfold and raise a tent trailer. Fasteners are unclipped, stabilizers lowered, wheels chocked, and sides pulled out. When all hardware was carefully rechecked for its correct position, the canvas sides cranked up and the door dropped in place.

The door is another nightmare of design. On older models the trailer must be perfectly level for the door to operate effectively. If the base is off plumb, the door will neither close nor open once closed. It's a lesson in patience at the end of a long drive to properly set a recreational vehicle in a camp space with aplomb. The arrival of new campers is often the entertainment of the day for the others in the resort. Camp stools are drawn up, drinks are poured, and chips opened so the audience will be nourished during the hilarious ordeal.

We were not immune. Yet, our first attempt to set the borrowed rig went surprisingly well. It was a wonderfully warm afternoon without a hint of breeze until the last item was unpacked. Deb and I had just opened a cold soda and complimented ourselves on our job. Suddenly a fifty mile an hour wind blew up the canyon like a jet. Trees started cracking, canvas was flapping, poles went flying. We heard and felt a big thump followed by the ripping of canvas, but couldn't move for fear of being hit by flying debris.

As quickly as the wind came up, it was gone. Later, we learned the extent of the storm damage. There were trees down and roads blocked. We patched the canvas sidewall with duct tape and went looking for the rest of our gear. After we gathered and reconstructed our rig, we laughed over the prospect of returning the tent trailer to its owner in a paper bag. Everything settled, we went fishing.

The friends we fished with were sturdier than our gear. Women enjoying their sixties and seventies, they could fish us younger gals to exhaustion. Flora was my college coach and mentor. During the iconoclastic years of youthful rebellion she got me out of more jams than I ever realized. She fought many skirmishes on my behalf in the privacy of her office. She won my vindication before I even knew I was in trouble.

She had invested so much energy bailing me out of scrapes, she decided to keep life-long tabs on me. She was my bulwark, a source of steadfast strength and encouragement as unconditional as motherlove. Montana was her summer retreat for almost forty years. Flora told us about Campfire Lodge, the privately owned resort on the Madison River where we came each year.

Jean was our elder stateswoman. She loved Montana so much she owned a house on Hebgen and parked her motorhome at Campfire. Jean was passionate about fishing, tied her own files, and was able to catch trout when no one else could. Jean served as a Womens Auxiliary Service Pilot during WWII and was the most fearless person I knew. She always wore a red hat over her silver hair making her easy to spot on the river. Both women were part of our Deschutes adventure a few years earlier.

For Deb and me it was an honor to share the water with such extraordinary women. Sometimes it was difficult keeping up with them as they worked the riffles and eddies. I most enjoyed the time spent sitting on the river bank adjusting our tackle while we talked. I never tired of listening to these women share their stories and suggestions. Nor did I weary of watching them fish. We named the tail of the big island upriver Flora's Point. She always caught fish there, and she looked so serene casting into the deep, smooth water.

Jean liked the challenge of scrambling over the boulders closer to Hebgen Dam. She usually managed to bring at least one trophy-sized trout to net when she fished this stretch. Always game for new streams, she relished a four wheel romp along a gravel track to any untried streams.

Pat was the Grand Dame. For many years a high school teacher and counselor, she was a patient listener and gentle soul. She fished occasionally, but her true joy was spotting new wild flowers and unusual birds like belted kingfishers, tying flies, or painting colorful scenes. Deb was more akin to Pat. If the fishing slowed, it was not unusual to find her painting beside Pat. Deb's drawings were always true and concise. Pat encouraged her to be whimsical and freer in her strokes.

The summer of 1995 was a stormy one. We spent long hours snug inside the tent trailer. Tanner, the cocker spaniel, was seventeen and getting very frail. Buster, the adopted dog, was happy to curl up next to Deb's feet while we played gin rummy waiting out a storm. We rigged a contraption to drain the rain from the awning. It became our routine to run out before the full force of a storm hit and collapse the screen room. We adapted.

Montana weather teaches many lessons. It changes your focus by bringing a clearer respect for simple strength to the foreground. Most of all you learn to laugh at yourself. Realizing how puny you are in the greater scheme of nature, a sense of humor becomes a survival imperative.

Imagination
walks an
unknown path
leaving
comfort in its
wake

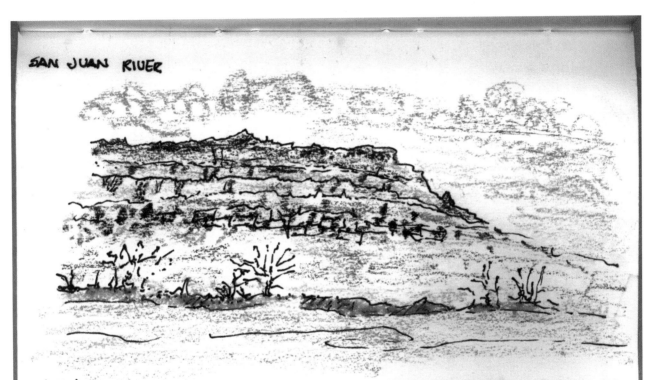

SAN JUAN RIVER

3/20/94
WE CELEBRATED SALLY'S 50TH B-DAY BY CATCHING OUR BIGGEST TROUT EVER...
WE HOOKED INTO 16 & LANDED 8/3. A GREAT DAY... HAPPY BIRTHDAY !/!

San Juan River

Fifty. Half of a century. Five decades. Two score and ten. The Roman numeral "L." How many ways can the big five-oh be described? There is little softness or cleverness or sweetness to it. For most of us the years speed by and the fiftieth is unexplainably upon us, there is nothing but dread hanging from it like Spanish moss.

It's not vanity, since our reflection in the mirror is the same as it was at forty-nine and our heart still leaps and soars at romance. The girl inside remains mischievous, just a little slower on the uptake and sporting fewer pimples. We boast of wisdom acquired from experience and patience learned from waiting. Yet the mere thought of a surprise celebration for this bitter-sweet milestone strikes terror in an otherwise fearless spirit.

I left town. Having already given myself a big, raucous party for my fortieth birthday, I was over such hoopla. Instead I was determined to fish as many of the best known western rivers as possible during the year of my fifth decade.

Early in the year and not quite fifty, I floated the Chetco River in southern Oregon fishing for steelhead. The most elusive of all the trout family members, steelhead are spawned in fresh water and swim out to sea. Returning to their birth waters to reproduce, they've learned wariness and stealth. Anglers frequently score zero when fishing for the dazzling silver swimmers. My guide was well known for his knowledge. A quiet gentleman who guided for President Carter, he knew the Chetco and worked hard to find steelhead. I had moderate success, boating three strong steelies during my two day float.

In commemoration of my own world debut I would fish the San Juan River in New Mexico, where the trout are legendary for their size. Fish are measured in pounds and yards, or so it was told. Many a fisher are so captivated by her giants their stories are told in hushed and reverent tones. I wanted to be as far out of town as March weather would allow and experience for myself the behemoths of the San Juan.

Deb and Tanner were the only invited guests for my celebration. We chose a famous outfitter, who offered accommodations, guides, and tackle shop. Not a fancy operation, the plainly printed brochure carried a photo of the ice machine — enticing for summer trips, but not quite as alluring during the winter. Nonetheless, they enjoyed an excellent reputation for both cleanliness and friendliness.

We rumbled across the Mojave Desert in the red van admiring the turquoise-colored trailers popular with desert residents. Climbing up to Flagstaff, Arizona and on to the big Navaho Reservation, through Tuba City and past historic rock formations we cruised. We drove in country famous in cowboy movies. Turning east where four states meet, Colorado, Utah, Arizona, and New Mexico, we rolled up to Navaho Dam out of which the San Juan River spills. To our disappointment we counted over twenty anglers in the first stretch of water just below the dam. Crowded conditions for March, I thought.

Hopscotching along the river, we stopped and considered the fishery. The water was murky brown and the banks were sandstone with wispy sparsely foliaged willows. Not at all the evergreen surroundings I favored. Pulling into the simple resort, we were greeted with head-turning stares. Two women, a big red van, and a cocker spaniel were an unusual parlay in this mostly male world. Even in the nineties, we were an oddity.

After unpacking and walking Tanner, we sauntered over to the tackle shop to learn everything we could about the local customs. Greeted warmly by a young woman, we began to feel more comfortable and were excited to go fishing the next morning. To honor my impending decade turn I spent a wad of cash on flies and other gear.

What I have failed to mention is the state of upheaval my hormones were experiencing. Deeper into menopause I could not have been. Instead of fishing I should have been banished to a yurt somewhere in Outer Mongolia. That is not to say I didn't have moments of geniality, but those were rare. Turning fifty didn't help.

My birthday morning was clear and cold. We met our guide in the crowded, smoky, tackle shop. As the only women, we had to jostle our way to the counter through some evil smelling, hung-over guys. An exercise which was working my cranky button hard. Our assigned guide was a part-time back-up, who rowed the river as an extra job. I was certain we got a leftover because of our gender.

"Lefty," our leftover guide, crammed Deb and I into his tiny, filthy Datsun with windows thick with smeary dust and ashtrays overflowing with cigarette butts. His disrespectful little rig sent my humor over the top of the ugly meter. I set my jaw hard, knowing if my mouth opened venom would spew.

We are driven to the famous Texas Hole, which was practically shoulder to shoulder with fishermen wading and casting from the bank. The water looked like chocolate milk, and I looked like Medusa. Snakes were shooting out of my head, and my thoughts were dark and vicious. Deb sensed my extreme displeasure and used evasive tactics to keep me from hurting Lefty.

When at last we were afloat on the river, Lefty rigged my rod and gave it a trial cast. Surprised by the quality, he said, "Nice rod." After he rigged Deb's he said it again, as if women usually had poor equipment. My mood wasn't getting any better. Mr. Leftover Guide kept losing points.

Lefty maneuvered the driftboat into the line of boats circling through the Texas Hole like carousel horses. Each boat in turn would drift through the run and row back upriver to drift down again. I counted nine boats in the round.

We surprised Lefty again by each hooking a sizeable trout on our first pass. For the remainder of the morning we continued our skillful fishing, and Lefty finally realized our proficiency. He did not, however, win my affection. By the evening our reputation as accomplished anglers had spread throughout the camp. The stares had changed from amusement to awe.

Our guide the next day was respectful and expert. He was one of the best in the stable, which we deserved. A handsome, knowledgeable young man, he took us downriver away from the crowded water. Under his deft tutelage Deb caught a huge rainbow trout. The photo of her smiling face and trophy fish was used in a magazine ad by the Farmington Visitors Bureau to entice anglers to their community. I was content to enjoy the float and land a few sizeable trout. The vipers of the previous day disappeared.

The third day on the San Juan River we ventured out on our own. The wind was ferocious and my line wrapped around every willow branch in the vicinity. My moody snakes slithered back with a vengeance. I came within inches of breaking my custom-made rod over my knee. At that moment I found the good sense to take my ugly self off the river.

The San Juan River became my metaphor for menopausal angling.

Size didn't count for me. I would rather catch three-inch pan fish if the conditions were friendly than great huge trout if I was surrounded by crowds and ignorant attitudes.

It is the totality of the adventure which brings me joy. In the same way I let the complete experience of menopause take me. I chose not to medicate or soothe with drugs what my body was doing. What kind of teacher could I be if I didn't know the talk and walk it? I would neither return to the San Juan River nor relive the menopause years. Both experiences taught me what I needed to know.

Fifty was a turning point in the way birthdays marking the decades always are. After long hours of contemplation I realized, like many women of my age, I had made up my life. Our only role models were Donna Reed types, the perfect 1950's housewives. Smoothly coifed hair and ironed aprons did not match the civil upheaval we experienced, or the truths we so vigorously sought. For those of us who couldn't choose the traditional path, there were no heroines to copy. We stumbled on roads strewn with pitfalls and disdain. Even my passion for fishing was considered outlandish.

Through many trials and some horrendous errors I managed to reach my fiftieth birthday. Perhaps not gracefully, but certainly with what could only be called amazing grace, I came to stand solidly in my own life. Out of my own experience I had selected very good tackle, and I was confident it would serve me well.

The river flows along
like laughter
swirling
around rocks
like children
dancing

JACK'S STACK

JUNE 29
GREEN RIVER

I CAN'T
IMAGINE A
MORE PERFECT
DAY... GOOD
FRIENDS, GOOD FISHING
& MUCH LAUGHTER....
SPECIAL CONNECTIONS

Green River, Jack's Stack

Spend any amount of time around rivers and streams and you will soon come to know the oddball names for bends, islands, pools, or rocks. In the same manner Native Americans designated their homelands by using events or remarkable landmarks, the new Americans migrating westward followed suit. Unlike organized communities, where roads are clearly marked and universally known, in the wild there are no street signs. To tell a spouse or fishing partner where she plans to fish in case dinner gets cold or the boss calls, an angler must devise a place naming system.

By now every fishable water has been described in some fashion. Most original names are long obscured by the later English designations and rivers frequented with regularity are described anew by each returning fisher. When I grew up fishing Big Pine Creek in the Eastern Sierra Nevada we created new place names almost every year. My mother came close to drowning after falling into a deep hole upstream, and it became, "Marcy's Hole." A cousin landed a twenty inch long rainbow trout while fishing underneath a willow branch and the site was named "Pip's Tree." There was a German family who camped in the same site every year next to a prime trout hang-out, of course we named it, "German Camp."

Deb and I were constantly designating river sites. We favored people-centered titles, like Flora's Point, Stoney Flats, or Tanner's Island. Fishing other streams we learned the locales from our guides. Hat Creek included Carbon Bridge, Fall River had Zug Bug Alley, and the San Juan boasted of Texas Hole. Noteworthy on the Green River was Jack's Stack.

It was Odie's turn to plan our excursion. She chose the Green River in Utah. After fishing with nine women in Oregon and the following year with five in Montana, we decided to make it an annual excursion. Deb and I organized the first sessions of fishing fun, so it was only fair for another woman to have a turn. Odie picked the Green during a skiing trip to Park City, Utah. While shuttling from the Salt Lake City Airport to the ski resort, she learned their driver was a fly fishing guide in the summer months. An affable fellow and enthusiastic fisher, he had her drooling for trout by the end of her family snow outing.

Deb and I spent our usual time on the Madison, packed up the red van and Tanner Dog, and drove south to meet the group in Park City. Trish, Ethel, and Odie flew in and rented a car. Accompanying them was Irene, a business associate of Odie's husband and a newly converted fly fisher. After a rendezvous in Park City, the six of us and Tanner, drove east on Interstate 80 into Wyoming. Ethel rode in the red van, and the other three in the rental car.

Miles of high plateau sage brush country whizzed past as we cruised. Some higher peaks of eight thousand feet tilted up, but were not spectacular in my view. Turning south at Fort Bridger, the lowering sun was coloring the bluffs a stunning ochre. We began to climb into the pine forest of Flaming Gorge National Recreation Area and arrived at our first night's lodging an hour or so before dark. Log cabins, a restaurant, and lodge were grouped around a small lake.

By the time the rental car pulled up Irene, who sat in the front passenger seat and navigated for Odie, had earned the nickname "Shotgun." Trish was too long in the backseat and cranky. I led her to a small row boat, tossed in rods and tackle, and rowed out on the tiny lake to fish. There was a small hatch and a few rises, but we were mostly airing ourselves out after the long drive.

In the morning we gathered together for a trip to Dutch John, which consisted of a trailer park and Stop & Shop. It was the gateway to the Green River as it emerged from Flaming Gorge Dam. We were meeting our outfitter. It was hot, and he was late. There was a little grumbling, but we were being unusually patient. The women were away from their hectic lives and it was enough to make them happy.

When John finally arrived, he was a jolly fellow with a sunny disposition and a slightly tattered drift boat in tow. Pleasantries were exchanged and introductions completed. We followed him down to the river where the other two guides were waiting with their boats. Our gear was transferred to the drift boats and taken across river to our camp.

By the looks of the tents it was a thrown together operation. As a rule outfitters will have gear which includes matching tents and industrial strength cooking facilities. Our rag tag camp looked as if John had searched his uncle's shed for enough tents to shelter six women. Three dome tents of three different brands and sizes were precariously pitched on the sandy beach. Deb and I got the largest dome because we shared it with Tanner. Odette and Shotgun were assigned the smallest because of their collective size. Trish and Ethel would bunk together in the medium model. Our guides slept in other tent models pitched at a discrete distance three hundred yards upriver.

The kitchen set up was primitive at best. We stowed our sleeping bags in our brightly colored nylon domes, chose fishing partners for the day, and headed toward the boats. Generally, for guided fishing excursions, piscators are on the water at dawn. It was well past midday by the time we were casting into the Green River. John assured us the river was a late day fishery.

Odie and I went out in John's boat. I couldn't help liking the big guy from New Jersey. He had a ton of kids and wife to support yet he was living his passion. Fishing in the summer and skiing in the winter, he managed to feed his school of children. He tied on a big high floating Atomic Ant pattern onto our fly lines. The secret, he said, was to count to three after we saw the fly disappear into the jaws of a trout. Ha, there's an impossible act. You watch your big black and white fly floating along easy as pie when suddenly "Jaws" comes out of nowhere and takes it down. Then, you are supposed to count to three before setting the hook. Fat chance, you can't even breathe let alone count. My first instinct, as would be most fishers', is to set immediately.

John barely dipped his oars into the Green when my Ant was swallowed and like the proficient angler I am, I pulled the fly right out of the fish's mouth. John laughed and said, "I told you to count to three." Meanwhile, Odie in the front seat was into a sizable trout. I yelled for her to breathe, which you always must do for her. She played it briefly then lost it.

Odie was still mastering the technique of playing big fish. She was too anxious and tended to pressure the fish. This trip would give her the experience she needed to become a better angler.

Our first day we started from camp and drifted past the territory where Butch Cassidy and the Sundance Kid hid from the law. There were fish galore and big ones. Rainbows to six pounds and brown trout as big as your leg were reputedly lurking in the Green. We fished hard for a few hours and pulled over all together for lunch on a small beach. Generally, when a group drifts a river, you seldom see the other boats during the day. The guides give each other considerable space on the water, so each boat of clients can be successful. During meal breaks are the only time the group meets.

While the guides barbecued and assembled our lunch, we women swapped big trout tales and laughed at our inability to count to three. I rigged my line in a method I learned during my exploits on the San Juan River. I waded out to fish. Two of the guides came down to the water and remarked as how my arrangement of flies would not work. As soon as they closed their lips on their last words I hooked a big rainbow. The fish obliged me by leaping three feet out of the water to show the boys the effectiveness of my tackle. Quietly, guide boys shuffled back to lunch duty. I like it when that happens, I mean I really like it.

Lunch eaten, we reboarded our drift boats and John rowed us back out into the Green. He was hugging the left bank and Odie and I were casting as close to the edge as we could. We were still using the very visible Atomic Ant pattern. As we drifted by a partially submerged log, John told me to cast to the small pool next to the tree trunk. I made a perfect cast, and was admiring my proficiency when a huge jawed brown trout gulped my fly.

Yikes! I said the world's fastest three count and set the hook. The giant was on. The brownie took off like a torpedo. I leaned into the knee braces and held on trying not to upset Tanner who was asleep in my seat. John was hollering instructions and rowing like mad to keep up with the fish. Odie politely reeled in her line and sat down to watch the action.

I wanted that trout bad. We hit some small rapids and John yelled he couldn't hold the boat any longer. "Get out," he bellowed, "go with your fish." Before the command looped through my cerebral cortex, I leaped over the gunwale and ran along the rocky bank rod high playing the big brown trout. I was all adrenaline and intention. I was mistress trout fisher. I was empress of the Green.

Slowly, carefully, I wore the brown out and John, who had anchored the boat, came running downriver with a net. He scooped her up and Odette snapped a photo, while we reckoned the size at twenty-four inches. Quickly returning the trout to the river assuring it was revived, we watched the grand fish swim away with a strong tail flick.

I collapsed. Laid waste by four pounds of fish, if I'd had a cigar, I'd a smoked 'er. It dawned on me I was a 50-year-old woman who'd jumped out of a boat to chase a trout. My, my, what a way to celebrate a half a century.

Even with my big brown trout, I wasn't the champion of the trip.

Ethel with her deliberate and steady style was the perfect angler for three count fishing. Every day she boated scads of trout. It was rumored she laughed hard enough to tinkle when her line became entangled about her boots while playing yet another huge fish. She was the guide's favorite, and apparently the trout loved her, too.

In spite of the tawdry outfit our meals were delicious and cooked for a woman's palate and appetite. Card games played under the light of the propane lantern were raucous. Tanner was a trooper. Even though he was sixteen years old, he would fish with me another summer. Shotgun fit like a glove, and she showed no trepidation fishing with our group of scalawags. Trish, however, grew more discontented. It was her last outing with us.

In the evening after a wonderful day of fishing we would find a quiet place along the river to bathe. It always felt ancient and primal to be with other women at water's edge cleaning the day from our bodies. The evening air was warm and caressing. The stars were bright and close. During our ablutions talk was hushed, as if in reverence for our sacred act. We all felt the communion.

As for Jack's Stack, I faintly recall a rather impressive boulder during one of the day's floats, but I couldn't say for certain. Deb and I never fished together on those float trips, so I don't know why she sketched it. I guess it was just one remarkable thing in an adventure, which was overflowing with remarkable things.

I went looking
    for a lover
and found
    passion
I went searching for
    a singer
and heard
    your melody

SEPT 7
PIT RIVER
BEAUTIFUL RIVER BUT
TOUGH TO FISH... MICHELLE & MARY
ARE IMPROVING DAILY... ODIE & I
TOOK A WONDERFUL WALK DOWN
RIVER... ALL IS WELL WITH
THE FIVE PESCADORES

Pit River

Anyone who has ever been tumbled by an ocean wave knows the power of water. The overwhelming force will turn a body in somersaults and slam a sweet face into the sand with equanimity. Fresh water is just as strong. Consider the churning terror of big, white water river runs, where even the most expert of rafters will haul their vessels on their own backs to avoid the treachery of the water.

Thousands of years ago emerging man realized the utilitarian value of water. It was not just for drinking, bathing, or fishing. The moving liquid was put to work. Waterwheels ground wheat and pumped other water; canals irrigated fields and refreshed villages. The cleverest idea of tumbling water past turbines to produce electricity popped up along with Thomas Edison's exciting invention of the light bulb.

So it came to pass, rivers were dammed for mill ponds or controlled storage. Man seeking domain over the power of water purposely entrapped the fluid for his own needs. Creeks and rivers were wrenched from their own paths of least resistance to flow through the improvement of mechanics. Ah, progress.

The beautiful fresh waters of California are no exception. All but a couple of the State's magnificent rivers are dammed for human needs. A water once captured becomes the property of someone or many someones. Usually utility companies own the water for use as power generation. The pristine flows of Northern California are interrupted by scores of small hydroelectric power stations. Most were constructed in the early Twentieth Century to bring light to the emerging populations of San Francisco and Sacramento. Beautiful in the simplicity of operation, these small turbines crank out inexpensive electricity like hummers. Much to the financial delight of the utility company and their stockholders, the return on their investment is substantial.

Under pressure from environmentalists and anglers alike, utility companies were forced to make some concessions to nature. Working together, the disparate interests made headway in improving the riparian habitat. Of course, neither side was totally satisfied, but the compromises were acceptable solutions.

Admittedly, my interests straddled the fence. Employed by a utility company I felt a certain allegiance to the corporate line. On the other hand, as an angler, I was ashamed of the conditions caused by hydroelectric generation; a similar quandary as biting the hand which feeds me. Information is the best remedy, and I spent long hours in research.

For my study methodology I chose fishing. Not so strange when you think about it. I would have first hand physical knowledge of the waters in question and could see the situation for myself. The existence of big, feisty trout in the same rivers and streams was a contributing factor.

As unlikely as it may seem, the northern quarter of California is relatively sparsely populated. The country is far from any industrial or commercial center and contains some very rugged terrain. Particularly, the northeastern section of the state, cornered by remote portions of Oregon and Nevada, is not a through route for any interstate highway. Travelers must cancel the cruise control mode of driving and traverse one-lane roads shared with logging trucks. Neither the roads nor the country are for sissies.

Out of the dramatic peaks of the northern Sierras and the southern portion of the Cascades flow the tributaries of the Pit River. Dammed below the co-mingle of Hat Creek, the mighty river becomes Lake Britton. Released again below the lake to reassume its identity as Pit River, the water has several power houses along its course both above and below Lake Britton.

On this research field trip Deb and I gathered friends to help us with our field observations. Odette, Mary, and I drove the five hundred miles in the red van with my aging cocker spaniel, Tanner. Michelle drove up by herself from Cambria.

Deb was spending the previous week visiting her parents in Redding, which was sixty miles southwest of our field of study. She borrowed their motor home to house our guests in relative luxury at the state campground near Burney Falls. Tanner, Deb, and I would sleep in the van as always.

Michelle and Mary were greenhorns to the sport of fly fishing. Michelle heard about our exploits and wanted to fish with us. She was a brave soul who made the long journey to fish with complete strangers. With her she carried wonderful treats from her wine shop in Cambria.

Mary loved adventure. As a travel agent, she could indulge her zest for experience. To my surprise she was game to learn to fly fish. Deb and I loved teaching the sport to our friends, so were always ready to organize an excursion. Odie never turned down the opportunity to cast to trout. So our little group assembled in the campground and prepared for our angling foray.

First, we needed a knot tying refresher lesson, which was accompanied with delicious snacks. Home-grown tomatoes with fresh basil, mozzarella cheese, and extra virgin olive oil were the perfect tackle assembling appetizers.

As the afternoon lengthened and the insects preferred by trout began to fly, we piled into the van for an evening's fishing at Hat Creek. Within an hour we were slipping on our waders below Powerhouse 2. Mary was wearing Deb's red fishing vest and looked very stylish. The trout liked it, too, and she hooked a small fish almost immediately. I stayed close to her assuring her tentative casts were adequate for her first attempts and coaching her about line drift. The others dispersed along the downstream bank.

The evening darkened quickly as it was late September, and we drove back to camp under a star-jeweled nightsky. Using the opulence of the motor home, we prepared a wonderful meal of crusty bread and tossed Caesar salad. The wine drinkers enjoyed a Central Coast Pinot Noir while we planned the next day's outing.

Just minutes from our campsite the Pit River flowed out of Lake Britton. After breakfast and an abbreviated casting lesson, we loaded into the van for our next fishing adventure. We drove across the dam and dropped down on the road next to the river. Finding a likely stretch, we parked and assembled our gear.

The Pit was a tougher water than we planned. Strewn with big boulders guarding deep pools and steep banks, just getting to the water was a challenge. Once close enough to survey the stream, Deb and I realized the wading was too dangerous for our group to chance. Swift, rocky, and with sudden drop-offs, we needed to keep everyone within shouting range in case of stumbles or missteps. We positioned the new anglers where they could practice their casts and line control.

There were no fish rising or insects hatching, so Deb soon lost interest. She and Odie decided to reconnoiter down stream in search of better access. I stayed with Mary and Michelle coaching them on technique and retying their tippets and flies. No hours on the river were unhappy or fruitless. The scouting party returned to report the bank steepened downstream and was even more difficult to fish. We chose lunch.

We fished calmer waters in the afternoon. We drove to a smooth, slow creek, which we waded all to ourselves. A creek so benign it allowed Mary to take a big fall and emerge without injury or fright. She splashed so quietly the only reason we knew she'd tumbled was seeing her hang her wet red vest on the fence post to dry. Undaunted, Mary went right back into the water after spotting a few trout.

Coincidentally, our trip to fish the utility company owned waters was an interval during which the same company was offering an early retirement option. I was eligible and ready. The choice presented some very scary unknowns, not the least of which were the financial considerations. Like the treachery of the Pit River, the offer came with many large life boulders and sudden bottomless pools. To accept an early out I needed courage, similar to fishing Pit River. I knew I wanted to fish, but was I willing to risk the cost?

Fishing with other women always boosted me in unimaginable ways. Watching them take to the water with sturdy intention, leaving their comfort zone far behind, gave me the strength to say yes to an undetermined future. I opted to take the pension and go fishing.

The Pit River remains for me the symbol of my own liberation. In a way the water and I were both controlled by the interests of others. Unlike the stream I had the ability to seek my own course. Although, there may come a day when the power of water may prove again to be stronger than the whim of man.

Tall conifer
against your rugged trunk
lean
fragile memories
within your evergreen boughs
echo
women's voices

9•6•93
MAMMOTH
LAKES

TWIN LAKES

SALLY, LUCINDA & I ARE ENJOYING OUR LAST SUMMER
VACATION. ABBY & T.O. ARE IN HEAVEN... SALLY, T.O. & I ROWED AROUND THIS LAKE
IN A.M. FISHED UPPER SAN JOAQUIN RIVER THIS AFTERNOON, LOTS OF LITTLE ONES.

Mammoth Lakes

Like no other place, the Eastern Sierra Nevada mountains evoke wonderful memories of my childhood. This rugged range strides down through the State of California like a team of young buck cowboys. Brave, lean, and uncompromising the craggy peaks grow taller every year. Formed by some geological event in the Pacific, here the Earth's crust shoulders up beneath California causing Richter Scales to shudder, marking continuous motion.

In the crystal clear streams tumbling down from melting glaciers, I first dipped a line weighted with split shot and hook wound with wiggly worm. Eight years old and already proficient at catching kelp bass off the rolling gunwales of sport fishing boats, I came with my family to fish for trout.

The trip was a long journey from Los Angeles. Roads were single lane macadam tracks and cars were unsophisticated machines prone to simple difficulties. Radiators bubbled over. Or the mysterious malady called "vapor lock" would bring our 1947 Ford to a hiccuping halt. After one extended bout of the fuel line blockage, which resulted in a six hour trip lengthening into twelve hours, my father relocated the fuel pump. He installed it in the trunk of our two door sedan in hopes of cooling the gasoline. Miraculously his simple idea cured the problem, although the pump made a curious ticking sound when the Ford was starting, which unnerved most passengers.

The solution to an overheated radiator was the water filled burlap bags with cork stoppers my dad hung on the bumpers. Since Dad was a telephone man, our bags were embellished with the Bell System logo, as were most tools in our household. The water in the bags cooled as we drove and could be used in the radiator, on the fuel line, or to quench the thirsts of passengers. Burlap flavored water was an acquired taste, but one that alerted the palate to vacation treats to come, like Spam and dried noodle soup.

On especially long, hard climbs when desert bags were emptied before the crest was reached, there were usually roadside springs where motorists could find water for their steaming autos. These areas were popular pull-outs, and cool spots for picnicking. There were no manicured rest stops with sparkling lavatories and specified pet areas. Lemonade stands built to look like giant yellow fruit were the travelers' oases.

Two hundred and fifty miles to my aunt's cabin on Big Pine Creek was a six hour drive. Since there were no grocery stores within easy access, the roof rack of the Ford was loaded with cartons of canned goods, peanut butter, and dog food. Consumables could not be too perishable.

In those early days an ice box was the only refrigeration, and the twenty-five pound block of solid ice was available at the gas station eleven miles down the mountain. It was purchased for a quarter at the white rectangular building next to the garage. You could hear the blocks rumbling deep within the wooden structure. The ice block came shooting down an interior ramp and slamming out through a square opening protected by a piece of canvas tacked over the hole. We kids thought it was the greatest machine and jostled for a turn to slide two bits into the steel slot.

Our vacation in the Sierras lasted the entire month of July. The dads would bring the women and children, stay a few days to fish, then drive back to the city. All of the kids, an assortment of cousins, enjoyed open access in the mountain playground. Fishing or playing cowboys, the days were wild and free. The women loved their freedom to fish, wear their hair in bandanas, and forget their usual drudgeries.

I grew up fishing with women, so it was natural to seek women companions with whom to angle. After my mother and aunt died, many years passed before I could find the will to return to Big Pine Creek. The cabin was gone. Destroyed by an avalanche during the two women's lifetime, only a weed infested drive and flat spot on the mountain slope marked the place of my childhood joy. Two tall pine trees where we had leaned our fishing poles still stood guard over the site. When at last I returned, I sat on a familiar bolder in silent reverie. After some time I said a prayer of thanks to the sisters, and wept.

Several years passed. Lucinda was living near Sacramento and discovered the breathtaking beauty of the Eastern Sierras. Deb was familiar with the Western Sierra, which was very different geographically. It was her first view of the magnificent crags of the eastern slope. We traveled across the high Sierra in the red van.

The Sierra Nevada range is home to Mount Whitney, the highest peak in the contiguous United States. Over fourteen thousand feet above sea level, it rises sharply from the high sage plateau of the Owens Valley. There are many majestic tors along the range, which can only be seen from the eastern side. They erupt from the plain like fierce sentinels, still snow covered in August and ominous in their powerful beauty.

The passes from west to east climb to nearly 10,000 feet above sea level. All but one or two are impassable during the winter months. We climbed over the Sierras on Sonora Pass. One of the most scenic routes, it is a steep ascent which then slips down to connect with U.S. Highway 395 north of Bridgeport. A stunningly scenic road, we followed it south past Mono Lake diminished by the minaret crags to the west. We met Lucinda in Mammoth for a few days of fishing the Eastern Sierra waters.

It was late in the season and most vacationers were gone. We found a campsite at Twin Lakes and slowly settled ourselves in the nine thousand feet altitude. Air was thin and a small stroll left us panting. We walked the dogs, Tanner and Lucinda's yellow lab Abby, down to the lake. There were fly fishers in float tubes terrorizing fish. Smugly we criticized their technique.

Deb and I rented a row boat, loaded it with snacks, gear, and the old cocker and rowed around the lake in search of big trout. My rowing was strongly right armed and caused the boat to glide in a circular fashion, but we managed to chase anything with fins and gills to the far banks. Tanner stood resolutely in the bow, ready to chase off errant waterfowl.

The following day we drove higher up the mountain to the headwaters of the San Joaquin River. The major tributary of the Sacramento Delta, its water eventually flows into the Pacific Ocean through San Francisco Bay. It was difficult to imagine this small creek we camped along became the mighty river of the Central Valley.

At some points the river was less than ten feet across. The weather was warm and we were fishing in shorts. Deb and I walked softly and carefully upriver taking turns casting along the bank or in small pockets of water. Using Deb's favorite dry fly, the elk hair caddis, we could only make one cast to each spot. Every few attempts would bring a small trout up from its hiding place for a hard take.

The fish were small, but energetic. If the set was missed there was no second chance. We ambled up river a mile or two happy with small results in the amazing country. A few diminutive golden trout, California's native species, took the elk hair pattern. They were a brilliant reddish gold color with prominent circular configurations on their sides. Golden trout are not known for size. Their environment is harsh and the feeding season short. The trout are prized for their natural origin and delightful coloring.

Lucinda spent long hours in solitude. Her high level corporate position kept her tuned very tightly. Any opportunity to be in the Sierras was a health-restoring treat for her. We returned to camp and found her reading happily sitting next to the river. She and I learned the sport together, but I made more time for fishing.

Above Mammoth Lakes we were many miles north of Big Pine Creek. It flowed down the granite tumble south of the long, slow, climb of Sherman Grade. Even my aunt's Cadillac would creep on its deep grind. Still further south than Bishop, the cowboy town famous for its Mule Days Celebration, the cold, crisp waters of my childhood creek washed past feeding trout. We wouldn't visit the ghosts of my youth this trip.

Being anywhere in the Eastern Sierra Nevada was occasion to spark those sweet memories. I couldn't watch my fly line float along a tiny riffle without recalling the pungent smell of the salmon eggs I used for bait or the taste of burlap in my drinking cup. Most of all I was certain I could hear my mother and my aunt laughing above the noisy rushing of the stream.

A friend came to me
whispering secrets
like a dandelion
blown naked
by the wind
I was filled

7-4-96

We took Mary to Bozeman,
she had a great time!
She's become
quite an
angler!

Buster is doing
much better after
a scary morning of sad raisin eyes! He wore himself out! the
secret is to keep him on his drag-a-chain! He's content to lay in
the river & watch us fish ... Sally landed a whopper today... 20"+
rainbow. Took her half way to Ennis. We had a wonder sing along
w/ Pat, & Flora's family. 4th celebration at Michaels.

Sally across
from Flora's Pt.

Sally Across From Flora's Pt.

Rain. More rain. Still more rain. Winter of 1994 ended the years-long drought in Central California by bucket-loads. El Niño, as meteorologists call the weather pattern, was drenching the middle of the state and warming up the Pacific. At first it was welcome. Now, too much of a good thing was too much.

Small communities were drowning under eight feet of water. Neighborhoods were inundated and small cars were washed off the highway. Worse yet, trout streams were raging torrents and would be unfishable for months. Besides all that, my aging cocker spaniel would not go outside in the rain. Tanner, the black cocker spaniel, was 16. A miracle of modern veterinary science, the dog was rickety but mobile. He was also very stubborn.

After four days of constant rain, during which I was certain my little red car was going to be swept to the ocean, a small patch of blue sky signaled a long awaited walk for Tanner and me. Deb went along on the airing, but the slow pace made her itchy. She usually left us behind as she went off at quicker speed.

After so much rain, it was amazing there were any smells left for a dog's nose to discover. Tanner was deaf and his eyesight dim. His smeller was as good as it had been as a pup. He was earnest in his sniffing maneuvers, and I was content to amble along on the other end of his leash.

Deb predictably was a quarter of a mile ahead of us. I watched her suddenly run across the street heading for an overgrown area near the railroad tracks. She hollered something in my direction, which I couldn't make out. Truth was my hearing was only slightly better than my black dog's. Slowly, Tanner and I drew nearer. I saw a large white movement and heard a high pitched bark.

Standing on the other side of the street, I watched as a furry white dog came toward Deb's outstretched hand. He was talking to her. A wrought iron fence separated the two. The dog put his head between the bars and licked Deb's hand furiously. She coaxed him to an opening in the fence, and he emerged wagging happily.

As the two walked toward home, the dog still talking and nipping Deb's hand, a thought whizzed by me like a news flash, "Deb has a new dog." Tanner and I strolled along behind them.

A good combination of Samoyed and Australian Shepherd, the white dog was perky and smiling. "I saw the white fur and thought he was a big stuffed toy. He was lying under the bushes and came right to me," Deb explained. Closer examination revealed a temporary tag from the local shelter. It was a holiday weekend and the shelter was closed, so he would be a mystery dog for a few days. We dried him off and fed him.

Deb called him Buster. He never left her side. Tanner was unperturbed by his presence, as if he knew his own days were numbered and Deb would need consolation when his time came. A few days later Buster's story was revealed.

He escaped from the shelter with his mother. She returned after a couple days. Buster eluded all capture attempts for almost a month. Kind souls in the neighborhood left food for him, but he refused any offers of sanctuary. Maybe he was waiting for Deb to find him, or he just got tired of the rain. Whatever the reason, he chose her. As a prelude to our water-based adventures, Deb brought him along on a canoe paddle in Morro Bay. He lay quietly in the bottom of the vessel happy to be near her.

"He'll do fine in a driftboat I think," she said referring to the float trip we planned for the summer. And he did. He became an integral part of our fishing trips whether we were wading or floating. His only fault was he didn't know when to quit. He would run until he was exhausted and then need a day to recover. The vet found a weakness in his hips, but compared to Tanner he was spry and energetic.

As long as he was with Deb, his life was happy. He had an irritating habit of eating out of the recycle tubs, which he must have developed while living by his wits. Buster could also grab a sandwich out of a hand before you could get it to your mouth, which was another skill acquired during his vagabond days. We reckoned he begged from the workmen building houses in the neighborhood when they ate their lunch.

By the summer of 1996, Tanner was gone and Buster enjoyed the privileges of solo dog. Not aggressive like the cocker, he would go out of his way to avoid canine confrontations. He became a campground favorite with his docile, independent nature. When Mary flew in to fish the Madison, she became another person in his herd.

I felt lost without Tanner that summer. Not yet ready to find another fishing dog for myself, the summer trip would belong completely to Buster. He did his best to shepherd us, but he finally pooped out during Mary's visit. Deb fretted. As vocal as Buster could be, for one entire day he was quiet and listless. There was none of the usual sparkle in his eyes. Deb was as sad as Buster looked.

It was always wonderful to have friends join us for fishing in Montana, but saying goodbye when they left was difficult. After bidding adieu I usually retreated to the river for solitude. When Mary left to continue her trip to Florida, I sought the Madison for comfort. Buster was up and wagging again, so Deb felt better, too.

We took the short hike upriver to Flora's Point. I waded across stream above the island where we buried Tanner's things. I began casting upstream to a big tailout below a smaller island. The water darkened into a deep pool and I saw a sizeable trout working the morning caddis hatch.

Without a trace of breeze my presentation of the big, buggy, orange bodied Stimulator was delicate and gentle. It barely kissed the river's surface then disappeared in a flash of shiny trout spray. I raised my rod tip and felt the barbless hook set. Playing out the slack line off the water, the fighting fish shook its head and raced for the current. I was hot after her.

The beautiful rainbow trout came flying out of the river with a vengeance and I let go a shrill yelp. She was a big fish and I was determined to hold her. After a few spectacular leaps, the trout turned down river. My reel was screaming. I sloshed to the bank to get a better angle on the racing fish. Running over the rocks, stumbling over tree limbs, scrambling over boulders, I chased the trout down stream. After several exhausting minutes she slowed and I reeled in madly, bringing her steadily to me against the strong river current.

Finally, the fish was near enough to net, unhook, and revive. With the discreet mark I'd made on my rod I measured the trout at just over twenty inches. Cradling her smooth body I returned her to the river. She regained her strength quickly and slipped off into the dark waters of the Madison River.

The excitement over, I sat on a sun-bleached log to regain my own vitality. My heart was thumping strongly and my lips tight from smiling. I had to calm myself enough to find my way back across the water. Pursuing the big fish I'd raced a hundred yards down the river. My legs were wobbly. I had to muster all my reserves to wade the current. Landing a fish that size would suffice for this morning's outing. I was content to return to camp, if I could first make my way back through the river.

While I recuperated I watched Deb and Buster work the quieter water across stream. Their energy blended in an unspoken duet; woman and dog together in sweet harmony. My heart ached for my missing dog, Tanner. Observing those two, I was convinced dogs choose their masters. They know before we do when a perfect match is made. Unlike us, their commitment is for life.

Happy souls
play endlessly
in sunlit meadows
then look up
smiling
as we
approach

7-11-96
Tanner Dog's final
resting spot...
Tanner's Island
on Flora's Pt.

We gave T.D. back to Mother Earth... the Osprey watched over us...

Memorial for Tanner
A Black Cocker Spaniel

We see each other with hopeful eyes. As human beings we can only be what we are. Dogs, on the other hand, possess the extraordinary ability to be how we want them to be. I wanted Tanner to live as long as I did, and he knew it in the magical way dogs understand humans. He tried with all his waning strength to be the perky pup I wanted during his seventeenth summer. When our photos were developed, it was sadly apparent he was slowly drifting from us. The camera didn't lie.

In October of 1995, the spirit of Tanner, a black cocker spaniel, left its body while Deb cradled the dog in her arms. The vet gently removed what was left behind. We grieved the deep mourning of heart friends.

Deb constructed a small wooden box. Inside we put Tanner's collar and a few bits and pieces of his memory. She carved his name on the top, and nailed it tightly.

The following summer we found a spot on his favorite island in the Madison River and returned his memory. When the last rock was placed to mark the site, we sat back on our heels and howled as Tanner had done whenever a trout was hooked. All the while, Buster crunched happily on a dead fish.

Elegy

We honor the life of a powerful warrior, a hunter, a lover, a dedicated friend.

A loving spirit whose devotion was stronger than his body.

Whose abundance of delight to be with us surpassed his energy to thrive.

Our lives will forever carry his impression and his paw prints strike with each of our steps.

We deliver his worldly possessions to the place where his joy was so exuberant that his voice raised to the treetops and beyond.

We send his spirit to his next destination knowing that the place will be brightened by his happy existence.

We honor his life with ours.

We grieve for his presence.

We celebrate his journey to his new life until we meet again.

I want to see me
with your eyes
to be the mirror
of your soul
the window
to your
heart

7·1·97
HENRY'S FORK

Our 10th year in Montana!
SHE'S AS DAZZLING AS THE FIRST
TIME... JOEL & JEAN ON THE
HENRY'S FORK; CAMPFIRE FRIENDS,
SNOCK ARRIVES TOMORROW. SCOUT
& CUSTER ARE HAVING A DOGGY
BLAST! RAINBOWS ARE
BACK IN THE MADISON!

Henry's Fork

Joel was the boy across the street. My family moved to 76th Street in South Central Los Angeles when I was seven years old. He was the first kid to wander over to see what my brother and I were all about. A skinny, black-haired kid, he was a couple years older than I, and an only child. I jumped off the roof of his garage once and forever afterward wondered why. The landing was more painful than I had envisioned.

For the next 13 years Joel and I were on and off best friends. We played "three flies up" in the vacant lot on the corner, "hide and seek" until our mothers called us in to go to bed, and walked to the local theater on Saturday to catch the matinee. My father died my senior year in high school. While my brother was stationed in the Philippine Islands, Joel quietly looked out for me in his absence. He did the things a big brother would do. He fixed the clutch on the 1947 Ford, and drove me home from parties if I had too much to drink. When we were older we played chess for hours, smoking cigarettes and drinking coffee late into the night.

There was a time we were both social odd balls. We found refuge in our history and comfort in our unspoken knowledge of one another. Joel was part of my family. We both were attendants in my brother's wedding, and afterward I drove Joel to the airport to catch his plane north, where he lived with his new bride. Partying a little too long at the reception, we had to run through the concourse in our finery to make the final boarding call.

Joel tells people he learned to trout fish from me. As teenagers we stalked the pristine waters of the Eastern Sierras plunking salmon eggs and worms into the riffles for hatchery trout. While I lounged in the luxury of my Aunt's one room cabin, facilities out back, Joel camped in his old Chevy. He removed the back seat and spread his sleeping bag out in the trunk. He spent his starlighted Sierra nights nestled among his camp stove and cans of beans. We worked the creek all day and in the evening sat around his campfire sharing our dreams and our confusion about the paths of our lives. We practiced our fishermen's lies, too.

Time passed. His family grew, and my life turned colorful circles. We lost track of one another. Then one of those unpredictable, magical co-incidents brought us back together. I joined Cal Trout, an organization for the protection of the wild fishery in California. Perusing the leadership roster I found Joel's name on the list of Governors. I phoned him for a long overdue reunion. Even after reconnecting, it took several more years for us to share a stream fishing together again.

The Henry's Fork in Idaho was one of Joel's favorite rivers. He and his second wife, Jean, liked to stay in a rustic resort nearby and fish intensely during the few days they could manage away from their frantic schedules. Deb and I drove past the smooth enticing water of the Henry's Fork every year on our way to Montana. In our hasty excitement to arrive in West Yellowstone, we would stop at the fly shop in Island Park to buy a few supplies, walk the dog, and speed off. Never tarrying long enough to fish. When we passed the river on our return we'd be deadheading west trying to make Winnemucca before dark.

Year after year, Joel cajoled me in the way only fellow anglers can. He described exquisite evenings catching large trout while the sunset turned the sky into a blazing palette. Finally, he teased me to submission in the same manner he used to convince me to leap from his garage roof. We arranged to meet them at their lodging, dine together, then head to the river for the late hatch of large mayflies.

A man who could wax so eloquent about the river's gifts was somehow very vague about the requirements for our outing. He said offhandedly, "We'll park in the highway pullout and walk through the State Park about a mile to the river."

We ate a multi-course dinner including dessert and headed out in separate vehicles. Deb and I dressed in our light-weight waders, made sure the dogs had water, and locked the van. Walking through the long meadow in the creamed-colored evening was sweet and toasty. So warm when we reached the river's edge, we were soaked with perspiration. The air temperature was cooling quickly and it was apparent we made a poor choice of garb.

Henry's Fork was bursting with activity. Huge mayflies, called Green Drakes, filled the air and flocks of gulls were diving and swooping while trout splashed for the bugs on the surface. Birds and fish were after the succulent insects, and a dozen anglers casting rhythmically were hunting trout.

Joel and Jean slipped into the river and took separate paths to rising fish. Deb and I went upstream to assemble our gear. We pulled on our fleece sweaters to stem the chill. Silently, we watched the action, chose our flies, and merged into the cool Henry's Fork water. Deb kept close to the bank. Always more comfortable in the moving water, I waded across the river.

As I began to cast, I realized the inexpensive leader material I purchased through a catalog was performing like the cheap stuff it was. My casting was terrible. Every trout within range abruptly stopped feeding. Any chance at a trophy rainbow hooked, played, and landed in the view of my old friend vanished with the fleeing fish. Slowly, I began to move as far away from Joel as politely possible. Yet, in his enthusiasm for our long awaited angling togetherness he waded right along with me.

All the hours spent bragging about fly fishing were about to become just one more huge fish tale. Worse still was the possibility of losing esteem in the heart of a man whose opinion and affection I valued so long and deeply. I started a series of diversionary tactics, comprised mainly of constant tackle changes. My line was always in my hand and fly box opened. Tie on a fly, cast a few times, reel in, change flies, and repeat.

As usual, Deb rescued me from mortification. With a sky full of feeding gulls it was inevitable at least one stupid bird would mistake an artificial for a real mayfly. One of Deb's beautiful backcasts fooled a feathered diner and she hooked a shrieking gull. Mayhem ensued.

The bird was screaming and Deb was splashing around trying to grab the gull's body to extract the fly from its beak. Every angler within a quarter of a mile stopped casting to watch the circus action. Finally, after several chaotic minutes the bird was free and the show ended. She called out to me that she was very cold and the dogs were overdue for a walk.

"Oh, goody," I thought, "a great escape mechanism." I reeled in my line and hollered our thanks to Joel. Deb and I sloshed out of the river leaving Joel and Jean still fishing.

We were Popsicle cold by the time we reached the red van. I cussed at my cheapskate heart all the way back, while Deb just shook her head at my foibles. I wanted Joel to be impressed by my fly fishing prowess, to beam in awe of my championship skill. Most of all, I wanted to hook a beautiful, big rainbow trout on the Henry's Fork while my old friend watched in appreciation. Instead, I made oafish attempts at presentation with a line refusing to dance. The harder I tried, the poorer the results, which was a fundamental error in casting a fly rod.

Warming up as best we could, Deb and I stripped off our waders and let the dogs out for a romp. We drove back to Montana with the heater blasting. There would be no bragging about the outing on the Henry's Fork, except in praise of the dinner and the company.

The following day we drove into West Yellowstone to shop. We stepped into the Book Peddler for a latte. As we stood at the counter waiting for the foam to steam a fellow said to Deb, "Aren't you the woman who caught the gull last night on the Henry's Fork?"

We laughed uproariously. I wanted so badly to shine during our first outing on the legendary river, but Deb had stolen the spotlight with her aerial proficiency. She was the one who caught and released a trophy our first night on the Henry's Fork, even if it was a gull.

Paper ribbons
strung with
exuberance
fluttered on
aspen branches

4th of July

Late nite solving the problems of the heart with Snork, Kat, & Sally... Beautiful sunny morning along the Madison. Kat & Snork went rafting. Cyn, Steve, Sally, dogs & I walked to Beaver Creek... What a wonderfully special day! The dogs had a fine doggy adventure. Saw a moose, many birds, & tons of wildflowers.

Now we celebrate independence with 15 around Pat & Flora's camp!

Steve & Sally @ Quake Lake

Steve & Sally at Quake Lake

Among the physical concepts we learn to accept is the solidarity of the ground. Homilies are devised around the strength of the firmament. We say, "Keep your feet on the ground." "Be firmly planted." "Stay grounded." When the earth shakes, heaves, or rolls all our assumptions are shattered like the glass breaking around us. A loud rumbling strikes the deepest kind of terror in any one who has been rocked by the ineffable power of an earthquake.

California natives know the fear. My first recollection of a big temblor was the Tehachapi quake. Although the epicenter was 150 miles away, our chandelier swayed crazily at dinnertime. It was the early 1950s. My parents, smart about shocks, hustled my brother and me into a doorway to ride the roller out. Dad explained it was the safest shelter in the house.

Earthquakes figured grandly in my folks' romance. Mom and Dad met during the Long Beach quake in 1934. They came running out of a downtown Los Angeles building. After the initial quake public transportation was halted by electrical failures, so my father gallantly drove my mother home. It took him six more years to win her. Every tremor after, my dad's eyes would twinkle.

Whether or not the campers along the Madison River in August of 1959 were as savvy as my parents will never be known. On August 17, just before midnight the earth dropped almost twenty feet. The Hebgen Lake Earthquake measured 7.5 on the Richter scale. A force so powerful it sloshed the water in the lake creating giant waves, sections of the highway fell away, and a gigantic landslide crashed downward at one hundred miles per hour. The waters of the Madison River were covered by tons of rubble and a lake six miles long by almost two hundred feet deep was formed.

When the dust settled and the aftershocks slowed, twenty-eight human lives were lost. It took a month for the Army Corps of Engineers to open a spill way for the newly flooded area called Quake Lake. The destruction remains very evident standing as testament to the dynamic forces of our planet.

Life renews itself. The partially submerged tree snags of Quake Lake became perfect aeries for osprey and bald eagles. Moose feed along the shore, and river otters slide down the muddy banks in comic frolic. There are big trout cruising in the deep water, and the campgrounds are busy with vacationers. Deb and I are among them

Down river from our camp a gravel road winds narrowly close to the water. Where the Madison slows as it enters Quake Lake, the road is closed to traffic in deference to the nesting raptors. Walkers are allowed to continue along the lake. It is an easy stroll and filled with colorful wild flowers and animal sightings.

Thirty-eight years after the earthquake those of us camping along the Madison River are ignorant of the cataclysmic geological event that profoundly altered the river. We were here to enjoy the beauty, the fishing, and dramatic vistas of the Madison River Canyon.

Deb's old friend, Jenny, who she calls Snork, and Kat are new to fly fishing. Professional women in designer jeans, they bring a certain chic to the river. Jenny has lived in Hawaii for many years and moves with the casual looseness of the hula dancing she studies. She is always smiling and her hair falls easily to tanned, bare shoulders. There is a phantom hibiscus tucked behind her ear. Only I can see it.

Kat is tall, blond, and impeccable. Raised in a formal Episcopalian household, she has a seriously proper presence and is easy prey for teasing. The two have a recent passion for the sport. Deb and I help them develop their skills and love watching them gain more confidence on the stream. Our campfire conversations cover the lascivious to the ridiculous as they skip along the late night hours.

Steve is Flora's wonderful, handsome, gentle, Greek, nephew. He and his wife, Cyn, are new parents. They camped in a big dome tent next to his aunt's motor home. They've stolen a few days together in the mountains. Both love to fish in conventional style, but Steve was learning fly fishing. He was completely comfortable surrounded by women, and was at his best when playing guitar around the campfire with his aunt. In the mornings he would stroll by our tent trailer with a toothbrush in his hand. Stopping to chat it would be an hour before he made his way to the lavatory. The boy loved to gab and exchange pleasantries.

Scout, my red dog with the curly tail, was a new addition to the summer's crowd. Time enough had passed since Tanner went to the ethereal meadow. I planned a fishing trip to Canada in the late spring and felt uncomfortable traveling alone. Camping in the red van, a companion with shiny white canine teeth made me feel less apprehensive.

Size was important. Whatever dog chose me had to fit through my doggie door. The animal would be required to travel and live with cats.

Friends started checking newspaper ads, and Deb circled several for closer investigation. I was reluctant. A beloved pet can never be replaced, but I was ready for a pal on the stream. There were certain traits I wanted in any newcomer. The pup needed a little snarl, no pushover, rollover, pee-on-myself wimp for me. If I was intently fishing a stream I wanted a dog to watch my back and challenge any intruder. I went to the animal shelter. Deb and Buster accompanied me. First I picked a Queensland Heeler for her size, but when I took her to the yard, she jumped the fence. "Nope, not you," I thought and returned to the kennels for another candidate. There he was. Not overly anxious, yet alert and enthusiastic, his card read, "Loves kitties, and riding in the car." Perfect.

I walked him to the run. He stayed next to me. I sat down and the dog sat down, too. He leaned against my leg. I was toast. Deb brought Buster into the yard, and the two dogs sniffed together like littermates. Game over. I paid the fee, got his paper work, and took him home.

His name was a goofy moniker. I changed it immediately to "Scout" and we had a long heart-to-heart talk about my expectations. Three weeks later I loaded him and his new bed into the red van, and we took off for British Columbia. Our second day out we fished a small Pacific Coast river. Scout led my hike to the water and stayed close while I fished. We were a good pair.

During the course of the trip we visited various homes and camped in a variety of locales. We fished, rode a ferry up the coast of British Columbia, and took long walks along the peat bogs in Richmond. When needed, Scout showed a bit of a snarl. There were a few kinks to iron out. Both dog and woman had lessons to learn, but in those weeks together we gave our hearts to each other.

To say Scout loved Montana was a big understatement. He loved to fish, yet didn't spoil my water by swimming through it. People stopped to inquire as to his breed, I said without cracking a smile, "New Zealand Trout Spotter." When I tied him at camp he hopped up on the picnic table to survey the surroundings as if on sentry duty. In my mind he was a comic with a devilish sense of humor and fun. The dog made me laugh.

The fourth of July was a brilliantly sunny day. A big gathering at Flora's campfire was planned for the evening. It was a perfect day for a walk to Quake Lake. Steve, Cyn, Deb, Buster, Scout, and I loaded a few snacks in a backpack and strolled out of camp. The walking was dappled with photo opportunities and points of interest. Buster roamed and Scout played trail dog by continuously checking his troop. We kept a slow pace and stopped often to admire the beauty around us. Returning to camp we were renewed and exhausted.

As the sun faded behind the mountain, our group of celebrants found seats around the campfire. Steve and Flora were playing their guitars and singing old favorites. Scout was on our picnic table guarding the tent trailer. Buster lay at Deb's feet.

I looked at the faces of my friends sparkling in the flame lighted night and thought of those campers decades ago whose dreams were torn open by the upheaval of the earth. It wouldn't do to live one's life in fear of natural disasters. The hand of fate strikes in unpredictable ways.

I added my loud, off-key voice to the chorus of singers and said a silent prayer for our great good fortune to be together on this Montana night.

Metamorphosis
swims her
up
sunlight flies
her skyward
craving love
and
heaven

7-11-97

WE HAD A GRAND DAY YESTERDAY... STARTED OUT SLOW BUT ENDED WITH RENEWED CONNECTION. SALLY & I FISHED BY ONE ROD & TOOK TURNS FISHING & BEING GILLYS. STOCKED A BEAUTIFUL BROWN & GOT HIM/HER ON A FLY I TIED. WE HAVE SPENT OUR MORNING PACKING & CLEANING FOR THE TRIP HOME. WE HAVE HAD A WONDERFUL STAY... EXCLUDING LOCAL DRAMA! SAD TO LEAVE OUR SPECIAL PLACE & PAT & FLORA. BUSTER & SCOUT WERE GREAT... THEY LOVED THE MEADOW. OUR SCREEN ROOM WAS PERFECT, NOW WE HAVE TO FIX THE TRAILOR DOOR! SALLY LEVELED (?) THE TRAILOR ONE LAST TIME. ADIOS CIELO GRANDE

FISHIN' BUDDIES

Fishin' Buddies

This is a story of two women fishing. In itself it is an unremarkable tale and the women themselves ordinary. We came together sober. Facing a life without the dulling effects of drugs or alcohol, we made our decisions individually. We met shortly after closing the cap on the bottle for the last time and found renewed hope in sharing the pursuit of trout with a fly rod.

We each fished and drank for as long as we could remember. Now we entered the stream totally present, and with the trepidation that comes hand and hand with insecurity. There were so many things to be relearned in our untried new way. Could the sport hold our interest or would it tempt us to return to our old selves? My past experience warned me of the dangers inherent when alcohol and rivers mix. There were times I stood in the current after drinking too many beers and frightened myself by the folly of it.

I was nine years older than Deb and had been fly fishing for five years. I fished California rivers and creeks. Having grown up trout fishing in the Eastern Sierra, it was a natural transition to move from bait to artificial insects. I loved the sport, but there was no guarantee she would enjoy it as much as I did. It proved to be a false worry after her first experience on the river won her over completely.

We started fly fishing together in 1985. We both had been sober for a year. Ironically, instead of joining a twelve step program we chose to fly fish together for twelve years. Each year a step, each step a year, we were one another's sponsor on the river.

Deb, a draftswoman by trade, historian by education, and doodler by nature, began a journal in 1993. It was her intention to create a first person account of life as an angler by chronicling our trips. Her entries were colored pencil sketches capturing the essence of the day. Additionally, she wrote a short commentary along the margin of the page. Over time her drawings became more sophisticated and our fly fishing techniques also improved. Curiously, our personal strength deepened and our confidence grew with it.

When we first started fly fishing we noticed very few women sharing the river or the sport with us. We, in our own zeal, felt compelled to introduce other women to fly fishing. As years passed, we happily encountered more like us in the stream.

There were old friends with whom we joined to fish in particular locations, and new friends whom we accompanied to other waters. Of course there were the dogs. The black cocker spaniel, Tanner, and the newer furry companions, Buster and Scout, all added an important ingredient to the riverside life.

The sport brought us together with our friends in ways we never imagined, and these amazing revelations were included in Deb's journal. Within her remarkable daily notations we found deeper lessons in the small encounters along the trout streams.

In 1988 we added an annual trip to Southwestern Montana to our fly fishing itinerary. Just as each year brings people to different stations in their lives, every year, with our return to the familiar camp, there were changes. We were fatter or thinner, smoking or not, poorer or flush, happy, menopausal. There were new jobs, new schools, new outlooks. We didn't realize the trip commemorating our twelfth year fishing together was to be our last for awhile.

Our lives during the mid-90s were transformed in major structural configurations. I took an early retirement from the utility company. Deb earned a university degree and enrolled in graduate school ninety miles from home. Both of our lives were altered dramatically. We were learning how to live in unrestricted ways. I was writing, coaching, and fishing whenever an opportunity arose. Deb was a disciplined student impassioned with academia. She was also struggling with the tragedy of a fatally ill family member as her younger brother was slowly dying of cancer.

There was not one defining moment that led us to separate waters, but the compilation of changes determined the choices we were to make. In the past we could smooth the roughest patches with an expedition to an outstanding trout stream. The summer of 1997 was different. We fished and laughed together trying our best to make the tough complexities of our other lives fade into the background. Yet, the trip back to California was truly a journey back to reality. Our relationship would take different off-ramps.

The last day of any Montana trip was always a sad occasion. Striking camp and packing up meant saying good-bye to old friends and to the Madison River. We would be leaving everyone and everything that embraced us so warmly during our stay.

This trip was the maiden outing for the used tent trailer Deb purchased. She spent many hours modifying it for our comfort and we enjoyed its convenience. Except I was never satisfied with its position. At least three times a day I would crank one end up and the other down, reset the supporting jacks, dig a hole under one leg or jam a rock under another. All these machinations were an effort to get the cursed door to open and close without jamming. I never quite got it true.

After packing all day I went down river a short distance for one last outing. It was my own quiet way of saying adieu to the water, the fish, the eagles, and the wild flowers. Deb watched me fish from camp and un-packed her vise to tie a fly for me. She plucked a perfectly tied caddis from her vise and joined me in the river. It was a sweet little elk hair caddis, her favorite fly. She had been determined to learn how to tie one properly. The one she brought to me was perfectly executed.

I tied it to my tippet and waded to a small side stream. We saw fish taking flies off the surface and knew it was productive water. Deb volunteered to gilly for me. Staying next to my left shoulder to avoid being hit by my line, she whispered encouragement to me. I made a few casts and I hung her newly tied fly in a bush on the bank. My gilly dutifully retrieved it intact.

Finally I made the perfect presentation to a hungry brown trout and like lightening the fish grabbed the fly and flew straight out of the water. I played it carefully, landing it as quickly as possible, and returned it un-harmed to the water.

Next it was Deb's turn to fish and mine to gilly. I handed her my rod. We spotted a second trout and she cast to it with her usual finesse. The trout took her fly immediately and gave her a good run before its release. The evening began to close in and we fished until dark, taking turns with the rod and with gillying.

Fishing is not truly a doubles sport. When two people fish together they are seldom close enough to chat. More likely they are separated by at least one hundred yards of river, and look up occasionally to check each other's location and safety. This evening Deb and I enjoyed fishing truly together. We giggled like girls at our goofs and hoorayed loudly at drag free drifts or perfectly timed sets. We made the deepest kind of memory. We were at our best that evening, totally present in our shared moment.

The energy we created through our sobriety and with our fly fishing engaged and electrified whoever stepped within its circle. It encouraged others to be unafraid, to live with passion and abandon, and to take focus to infinity.

The entries in Deb's journal drew those lines and pictured the simple story of two women fishing. Her honest sketches captured the sweetness of friendship and easy camaraderie women create. Her drawings were also the inspiration for my prose and poetry.

Our fly fishing was not meant to stir the primal issues of man against beast. Nor was it considered a metaphor for any dark, sinister themes. It was a communion with our home planet and a reunion for unimpaired senses.

What we always intended to share was our exquisite experience. Deb and I hoped to make a connection with others yearning to live within their own joy. We wanted to encourage whoever we touched in the best way we could, as friends and fishin' buddies.

About the Author

Sally and Scout

A native Californian, Sally I. Stoner began writing poetry at age 15. Until recently, you could read her monthly articles in the San Luis Obispo Magazine. Her stories have also been published in *A Different Angle*, edited by Holly Morris, *The Women's No Nonsense Guide to Fly Fishing Favorite Waters*, edited by Yvonne Graham and the *California Flyfisher*. She is currently working on a collection of her poetry, to be published by K&D Limited, Inc. in 2001. When she is not fishing or writing she shares her knowledge as a flyfishing instructor for the California's "Becoming an Outdoors-Woman."

About the Illustrator

Deb with Buster

Deb J. Cox, M. A. lives in San Luis Obispo, California. A historian and an artist, she owns and operates a drafting service designing custom homes. Cox has a Master of Arts degree in Latin American History from University of California at Santa Barbara. A flyfishing instructor for the California's "Becoming an Outdoors-Woman," Cox has been fishing since she was two years old and fly fishing for the past 16 years.